FLIGHT AND REFUGE

Reminiscences of A Motley Youth

JOSEF EISINGER

For Styra, Alison, Simon, Sumathi,
Dashiell and Arlo

CONTENTS

INTRODUCTORY COMMENTS

These autobiographical essays were not conceived as chapters of a book at the time they were written; most of them were written several decades ago and were intended for family members and friends who were curious about my motley youth. The original impetus to write them came from my daughter Alison, for she, along with her brother Simon, has long had a keen interest in the history of our family. It is my hope that these recollections will put into context the various family yarns they have heard since childhood. The possibly misguided idea of bundling these pieces into a book occurred to me much later.

Telling stories to your children and grandchildren is the traditional way of transmitting family history, but since oral histories are notoriously unreliable after passing through a couple of generations, a written memoir provides a more reliable record. In addition, these recollections are also of some historical interest for they illustrate the profound changes that can take place in such an insignificant interval of time as a human lifespan. I have sometimes tried to imagine how the lives of my parents and more distant progenitors were affected by the social, political and technological changes that *they* lived through. Wouldn't it be nice, I thought, to be able to read *their* memoirs and to better understand the world they experienced? This was why I urged my father to set down his reminiscences, and although he filled only a dozen pages when he was ninety, they tell us something of his life and times. They appear in translation in Appendix I. Other appendices deal with the origins of his family, my parents' escape from the Nazis, and with my professional life, with my wanderings behind me.

The turbulent years of war and emigration I experienced as a young man shaped the remainder of my life. They left deep impressions and I can recall many incidents of those years with remarkable clarity to this day. Little wonder, that reminiscences of the years following the *Anschluss* are much sharper than the years of my tranquil childhood.

As far as the completeness of these reminiscences is concerned, a comment of Einstein comes to mind that I came across while working on *Einstein on the Road*. In the course of a conversation with a friend Einstein mentions the travel diaries he kept, and added that his most interesting experiences he had omitted, however.

Fortunately, I did not have to rely entirely on my memory in composing this memoir: I was able to consult family letters, as well as a diary I kept for a few years, beginning soon after emigrating. Naturally, I also made use of the reminiscences of my contemporaries, particularly, my sister Lesley Wyle, also my cousins Hannah (Hanni) Sherman, Frieda Redlich, Erich Eisinger and other relatives and friends, as well as books.

I am, moreover, the fortunate owner of several recorded conversations with my parents. I made them in 1967 when their memories were still fresh. They were transcribed and translated by Lesley and appear in her fine memoir *Preserving the Past*. On them they talked of their youth in Skotschau and Kostel, their experiences during WWI, their lives in Vienna, and of their dramatic escape from Nazi-occupied Vienna in the early days of WWII. I made the tapes on the Uher reel-to-reel tape recorder that Styra and I had acquired with the intention of recording Bulgarian folk music on our trek through the Balkans in our SAAB automobile (1965). It was a fascinating trip but the Beatles had already made great inroads and genuine folk music was hard to find.

This memoir sketches my life from birth to the end of my student days. While the chapters dealing with the subsequent seven decades remain unwritten, it is not because they were uneventful or lacked adventure, but the life they would describe is not atypical of that of an academic in twentieth century America. A few idiosyncrasies that hark back to my tumultuous youth did persist, however, both in our family's camping, hiking, sailing, and kayaking trips, and in our tangible environment. Our the thirteen acres of hardwood forest on Musconetcong Mountain in New Jersey, a homestead we call Cleehill, holds several wooden buildings and wood sheds that hark back to the carpentry and woodsman skills I acquired during my internment in Canada. We still heat the house with firewood that we cut and split each year, and when I hoe in our vegetable garden there, it brings back to me my farming days in Yorkshire. But at heart, I have remained a committed urbanite who feels most at home in our other family abode, Minetta Banks, a cozy 1820 brick building in Greenwich Village that we fixed up assiduously, in which we raised our two children and have inhabited for over fifty years.

Those unwritten, virtual chapters would tell of my haphazard search for a congenial niche in the strange New World I was transplanted into, on my own and still a boy; of coming to terms with youthful romantic, sometimes painful, episodes, and of the ups and downs of my professional life. They would also tell of my good fortune of winning the matchless and much-loved Styra as my wife and comrade, of creating with her our two homesteads, and of raising our splendid offspring – albeit, without me ever quite abandoning my solitary ways.

My life as a basic research scientist, which is sketched in an appendix, undoubtedly shaped my view of the world and of society which I have not tired of observing. It made me a confirmed skeptic who believes little without reliable evidence. My historical and biographical research drew me deeply into the lives of many fascinating personalities, ranging from Albert Einstein and Johannes Brahms to Beethoven and Eberhard Gockel, an obscure 17th century city physician of Ulm (of whom more in Appendix IV). They all had a prominent presence in our household, some of them, for many years.

But I stray from what is at the heart of this memoir: Where my life journey began, and the unpredictable circumstances that shaped its course. Looking back, it seems that I am apt to recall fulfilling periods more readily than the wretched ones – of which I had my share. My father also had a buoyant, optimistic and at the same time, fatalistic view of life that is reflected in two stories he liked to tell: In the first, a married couple comes to the rabbi and ask him to resolve their dispute. After listening to the woman's account, the rabbi declares that she is in the right; he then hears the husband's story and tells him that he is right. When a bystander thereupon asks how they can both be right, the rabbi tells him: you are right, too!

In the other story a traveler arrives at an inn in South Tyrol and rents a room for the night. Coming downstairs for his dinner, he witnesses the arrival of another traveler who also asks for a room in the inn. A little later the first traveler approaches the innkeeper and asks why he was paying 100 Kronen for his room, while the newly arrived guest was only charged 50 Kronen? The innkeeper shrugs, spreads his arms, and replies: *E fortunato!* (He is lucky!)

I, too, have been *fortunato*: Fortunate in that I and my immediate family survived Hitler and the devastating war, fortunate in looking back on a fulfilling professional life that provided financial security while affording me gratifying insights of our world; and fortunate in still enjoying reasonably good health after nine decades, and having been endowed for over fifty years with a splendid family, lately augmented by two grand grandsons, Dashiell and Arlo.

New York, 2013

Addendum

Having procrastinated for three more years, I am most grateful to An Diels for her kind help in turning this group of essays into a book, and to Alison and Simon Eisinger for their copy-editing help. Before putting it to bed, I take this opportunity to add a few words.

My two grandsons, now nine and seven, have reached the age of individuation – while I am still around. In years to come, they may even retain a distant memory of their weird grandpa, known to them as Papa, who used to pick them up from school, ride with them the trails of Cleehill in his old tractor, and who taught them how to make Wiener Schnitzel.

My second book about Einstein, Einstein at Home, has just been published – leaving a big hole in my daily "schedule". The work on the book brought me even closer to Einstein the man, as well as to the Mendels and reminded me of the extraordinary role they played in shaping my life.

Surrounded by a close-knit loving and busy family, I am increasingly mindful of acting a part in the last scene of the play. I still enjoy the part – often with gusto – though my joints are a little creaky and I hear the strains of Papa Haydn's Farewell Symphony playing off-stage.

New York, in June 2016.

1

CHILDHOOD IN VIENNA

MY FAMILY

I was born on 19 March 1924 and for the next fifteen years I lived at the same address in Vienna's Third District, at Reisnerstrasse 29, a graceful turn-of-the-century art-deco five-story apartment building. Its ornate entrance was flanked by pillars topped by sculptured angels (really puttis) and the tall, ornamental bronze-clad front door was so heavy that I well recall the proud day when, for the first time, I was able to push it open by myself. After the demise of the Habsburg monarchy at the end of the First World War, the influx of displaced army officers, civil servants and refugees from the Austro-Hungarian empire's vast lost territories caused a great housing shortage in Vienna, and Papa had been very fortunate to secure this spacious apartment in a desirable middle-class neighborhood, shortly after my sister Lesley (neé Ilse) was born (January 7, 1921). She was three when I made my appearance on Earth, and she had been told to put a cube of sugar on the window sill to attract the stork that would deliver her baby brother. Her first glimpse of me was in the Sanatorium Loew where she recalls seeing me in a lace-trimmed cradle with a nun wearing a huge headdress hovering over me. When Lesley asked Mutti why she was in bed in the middle of the day, Mutti explained that the stork had bitten her leg in the course of delivering me.

My date of birth has always had an odd significance for me, for I share my birthday, as well as my first name, with my grandfather Josef (nick-named Rüderer – one likely to cause a commotion) Eisinger, whom I never knew, but who was a somewhat legendary citizen of Kostel, the ancestral home of the Eisingers. The 19th of March is, moreover, the name-day of St. Josef, Mary's husband, known as Josef the Provider (in Austria, *Josef Nährvater*). The day is celebrated as a holiday in predominantly Catholic Austria, as it is in the Italian community here in New York's Greenwich Village, where on that day, Rocco's Bakery on Bleecker Street offers the traditional San Giuseppe zeppoles.

Now, while it is a tradition among Jews to be named after a grandparent (unless he/she is still alive), the name 'Josef' has specific historical significance in this case, for it derives from the enlightened Austrian Emperor Josef II, who emancipated Moravian Jews in 1782 and obliged them to adopt German family names. In that year, my ancestor, Markus Löbisch, who was born and died in the small Moravian town of Kostel, changed his name to Markus Eisinger which makes him the *Ur*-Eisinger. Two years later, a son was born to Markus and his wife Eleonora (known as Elkele) and not surprisingly, they named him Josef in honor of the Emperor – as did many other new Jewish parents of that era. This Josef Eisinger also spent his entire life in Kostel and was the grandfather of Josef (Rüderer) Eisinger of Kostel and Lundenburg, who was my grandfather.

Upon arriving on planet Earth, I joined a household that consisted of my parents, Rudolf and Grete, my sister Ilse (she changed her Germanic sounding first name to Lesley during WWII) and Ida Weihing, known to the family as Idi. She was our housekeeper, governess, cook, or what was then known as a *Faktotum*. By playing all these roles, she freed my mother to work in the family business, which was dedicated to importing and distributing sea sponges, chamois leather, loofahs, and other toiletry articles. As a result, I spent a greater portion of my early years in Idi's company, than in my mother's. One of my earliest childhood memories is riding on Idi's shoulders while she prepared the family meals, and so it was as an aerial observer that I acquired my basic knowledge of cooking and baking. While I may have been a keen observer, I chose not to speak until I was three years old (a reluctance I share with Einstein) which caused my mother sufficient concern to consult a specialist.

In spite of being a verbal laggard, I enjoyed playing the games of childhood and the mind-games that accompany them. Lesley reminded me of my fondness for my little *Leiterwagen* (rack wagon) in which I transported my only doll, Friedolin by name. I had enough railway tracks to cover the floor of the room that I shared with Lesley, and I treasured each new rail car for my train hauled by a spring-powered locomotive – electric trains still being a great rarity at the time. I also enjoyed playing with my Matador set, wooden blocks furnished with holes for wooden sticks which made it possible to assemble large structures, some even with moving parts. In the doorway of our room hung a punching bag, for I had developed an interest in boxing. I recall setting my alarm clock to 3 a.m. one night so I could listen to the radio broadcast from New York of the famous boxing match in which Joe Louis knocked out Max Schmeling in the first round. That bout had considerable political overtones, for the Nazis who were already in power in Germany (1936) had touted Schmeling as the personification of invincible Germanic manhood. Lesley and I both owned wooden scooters, called Tritons, and she was fond of playing Diavolo, a game of skill that was the current craze of all the girls in the park.

Growing up alongside an older sister is like having a personal tour guide to life, as I was able to observe in my own two children. When Lesley and I were little, our nightly fare was *Griesbrei* (semolina porridge) and as an incentive to eat all of it, Idi always put a piece of chocolate in the center of the plate, her idea being that you could attain that treat by starting to eat at the edge of the plate and spiraling in towards the center. At least that's what a good kid like I would do, but my older and wiser sister told me: "*Sei nicht so blöd, geh schnurstracks zur Mitte!*" (Don't be so stupid, go straightaway for the center!)

My father, Rudolf, was born in 1883 – a century after the Toleranz edict – in Göding, Moravia (now Hodonin in the Czech Republic); but the true family seat of the Eisingers since the 18th century is the nearby town of Kostel (now Podivin), some 50 miles north of Vienna. In the wake of the emancipation of Austria's Jews, Papa, along with other enterprising young men, was drawn to Vienna, the Imperial capital where opportunities were far greater than in the provinces. After completing his military service as a warrant officer in a Hungarian artillery regiment, he worked as a salesman for a sponge importing business, a job at which his personal charm helped him to excel. When World War I broke out, he was called back into the army and served at the Russian front. He was wounded and decorated with the *Tapferkeitsmedaille* (bravery medal) before obtaining a medical discharge in 1918 on the basis of an unconventional heart rhythm. Fortunately, his heart nonetheless continued to serve him very well for the next sixty years, and I hope to have inherited its finer features.

In 1912, when Papa returned from his initial three-year stint in the army, his employer reneged on his promise to make him a partner, whereupon Papa opened his own very similar business on the Rennweg in the Vienna's third district. The business flourished and before long, he was able to move to a prime location in the heart of Vienna's inner city, on Hoher Markt 12. When WWI broke out in 1914, he was recalled to the army, but he managed to keep the business going throughout the war, thanks to the help of his sister Mathilde.

At war's end, the vast Habsburg empire had shrunk to a tiny Alpine republic. Papa was approaching forty, and with seven years in uniform behind him, he was still single. A matchmaker brought him to the attention of the Lindner family who lived in Skotschau, Upper Silesia, as a good prospect for their daughter Grete. Reluctant to buy a pig in a poke, my mother-to-be took the train to Vienna and paid Papa's shop a visit, *incognito*. She purchased a sponge from him, and in the course of that transaction gained a sufficiently favorable impression of Papa to accept his proposal of marriage some time afterwards. They were married in the synagogue of her hometown Skotschau (now Skoczowa and in Poland) on December 30, 1919. The Lindner family's textile store on the town's market square was founded in 1820, and the Lindners enjoyed considerable prominence in Skotschau. Mutti arrived at her wedding ceremony in a carriage provided by the local Catholic priest, and the newly-weds spent their honeymoon in Germany. They visited Hamburg and several other German cities – a seemingly curious choice, for the young Weimar Republic was often in violent political turmoil and inflation was rampant.

Mutti was ten years Papa's junior. From an early age, she had played an active part in her family's textile business. Her childhood could not have been a joyous one, for she could not recall a time when she was not working. Even as a child she had been expected to help in the shop. By the time she was in her teens, she was in charge of selling fabrics from a stall in the markets of nearby towns, having traveled there in a horse-drawn wagon laden with bolts of cloth. When the First World War broke out and most men were called up to serve in the army, she was twenty-one and had the difficult task of locating and buying the increasingly scarce merchandise needed in the family business. For a while, she also managed a second shop that the Lindners opened in the much larger town of Teschen (Cziecin), 15 miles from Skotschau. Her mother was busy running the family business. and with her father, Leopold, Mutti and her five siblings had only brief, formal exchanges. She remembered him as someone very withdrawn and hard of hearing, to boot, and she had been told never to disturb him, because "*er hat Sorgen*" (he has worries). When I asked her what kind of fun she had during her childhood, she could think of nothing. Nor was frivolity her strong suit in her later life and it was a good thing that Papa's boundless optimism and good humor kept the scales of their life together in balance. Mutti never lost her sympathy for people in the selling trade, and all her life she found it hard to pass by a street vendor, knowing that she could brighten his day with a purchase.

During the First World War Mutti obtained the necessary official permission to visit her brother Siegfried, who was serving as an officer at the Russian front, about 100 miles to the east of Skotschau. She told me what a remarkable experience that had been, to be the only young woman among the army officers stationed in a war zone; she must have caused quite a stir. She lodged with a local Jewish family, but her liberal, German-speaking background had not prepared her for her much more observant hosts in Galicia – orthodox Jews who spoke Yiddish and wore kaftans and the traditional fur-trimmed hats.

With Mutti's business acumen and Papa's energy, charisma and specialized expertise – he took pride in being a court-appointed expert witness in cases dealing with sponges – their business prospered modestly even during the economically depressed nineteen twenties and thirties. Papa traveled throughout the Austrian provinces, as well as the territories of the former Habsburg monarchy that were now located in Poland, Czechoslovakia, Hungary, or Yugoslavia. I doubt that there was a toiletry shop or drugstore (*Perfumerie*) in Austria that he had not called on in the course of his travels. Occasionally, a mustachioed Greek sponge wholesaler came to Vienna on a visit, and Papa would comment jokingly that it takes a Greek to get the better of a Jew. The retail shop which was largely in Mutti's hands, naturally carried sea sponges (synthetic sponges did not exist) and chamois, but also perfumes, eaux-de-Cologne, hairbrushes, combs, loofah (luffa), corks of every size and shape, neatly arrayed in dozens of drawers, also washcloths, brushes and other toiletry articles, some that Papa had designed and were manufactured for him.

EARLY MEMORIES

As a boy, I enjoyed hanging out in Papa's store and it made me feel grown-up to be initiated into his trade. He taught me how to distinguish the different sponge varieties and where each came from, also, how they were cleaned, bleached and shaped before they were sold. The best quality sponges came from the Greek islands and they arrived in huge bales, so highly compressed that each sponge was quite flat. They were dark brown in color, and to my delight, they were accompanied by all kinds of seashells, dried sea horses and other marine life debris. While the shop had a certain exotic aura and I liked being there, I don't recall seeing myself following in Papa's footsteps, nor had I formulated any other plan for my future.

The shop was located on the Hoher Markt, the ancient square in the center of Vienna that was the site of the Roman camp Vindobona, some two thousand years earlier. During the Middle Ages the city hall had stood there and it was the site of public executions. The entrance to the store was almost directly underneath the famous Ankeruhr, an ornamental clock that forms a bridge between two buildings facing each other on a side street. The clock is a tourist attraction to this day, and every day, at noon, a crowd gathers to watch the procession of ornately colored statues glide across the clock face to a musical accompaniment.

The shop's office was a great attraction for me as a child. I was fascinated by its (mechanical) typewriters and the books with divider pages for keeping postage stamps and excise stamps of different denominations. I was an avid collector of postage stamps, as were most boys of that era. The two floors of the establishment that were below street level, known as the sous-terrain, housed storage rooms and workshops for processing sponges. After the sponges had been thoroughly soaked and washed, they were bleached to different hues of brown and yellow in large wooden vats with hand-cranked wringers mounted between them. (Since the hydrochloric and perchloric acid used to bleach them is not quite harmless, natural brown sponges will outlast bleached ones.)

I still recall the characteristic chemical smell of the sous-terrain workshop which was presided over by Herr Hoffmann who worked for Papa for many years. Papa instructed Lesley and me in the fine art of giving a sponge a pleasing shape by trimming it with shears without reducing its size unduly! His good-natured and easy-going nature concealed the fact that he was a perfectionist in everything he tackled. I can still see him holding a sponge at arm's length to scrutinize its shape and porosity with the critical eye of a sculptor. His favorite saying was *"Wenn schon, denn schon!"* which is equivalent to 'if it's worth doing, it's worth doing well'; another was *"aus Nix wird Nix"*, i.e. from nothing, comes nothing. Though he had only had eight years of formal education, he was an expert stenographer and bookkeeper, a rapid . arithmetician, and a some-time inventor.[1]

Papa's childhood in Zistersdorf may not have been much happier than Mutti's in Skotschau. At age ten he was admitted to a Gymnasium in Vienna, but was able to attend it for just one year, before his elder (and very erratic) sister Mathilde, with whom he lodged in the big city, sent him back to Zistersdorf to finish his schooling. For this, Papa never forgave her.[2] Papa's mother Anna was, I am told, very observant and widely disliked by those who knew her. I hope that his father, Josef Rüderer, offered some consolation, for he is said to have had the earthy good humor that is a hallmark of many Eisingers. His nickname, *Rüderer*, suggests that he was inclined to set off a commotion.

The shop was a 20-minute walk from our home in the Reisnerstrasse and Papa and Mutti usually came home for the midday meal, after which Papa always took a short nap, called a '*Napetzer*'. The mid-day meal was substantial and always included dessert, *süsse Nudeln* (thick hand-rolled noodles served with sugar, cinnamon, poppy seed, or nuts), *Kaiserschmarrn*, or *Marillenknödel* (apricot dumplings), but in the evening we usually ate a light cold supper with tea, bread and butter, cheese, sardines, or herring, followed by stewed or fresh fruit. On Friday nights, the usual Sabbath fare was *Eingemachtes*, goose cooked in pieces and served in a dill or mushroom sauce. All parts of the goose were used. The neck was stuffed and was eaten cold, in slices, while the liver was sautéed and thin slices of the cooled liver were consumed on bread spread with goose fat. The skin was rendered to yield cooking fat, as well as Papa's favorite snack, *Grammeln* (cracklings). Papa also loved that Viennese specialty, boiled beef, particularly the marrow, which he salted and ate on a slice of the Vienna's delicious sour dough bread ('*Ankerbrot*'), a delicacy I still miss. Papa was also fond of Penezl which is made by rubbing a slice of bread with garlic before lightly frying it in a little fat, a treat that probably harked back to his childhood in Kostel. And I share with him a fondness for *Milirahmstrudel*, a cheese strudel with raisins.

Our apartment in Vienna was just a few blocks from three public parks, and Lesley and I made copious use of them. I recall playing 'London Bridge is falling down' and 'Let us go gathering nuts in May' in the Modena Park when I was 4 or 5 and belonged to Frau Else Liebmann's 'Englischer Kindergarten' class. Mutti, ever practical, had enrolled Lesley and me, so that we would get an early start in a foreign language – she had all the right instincts for surviving in an uncertain and hostile world. When I was a little older I spent a lot of time playing soccer in the Modena and Arenberg parks, also in the Stadtpark, but the fenced-in playing fields with real goals which are there today, did not exist.[3]

I was neither accident nor illness-prone but I did contract scarlet fever twice, or at least, was diagnosed with it. I was very young the first time and, as was then the medical practice, I was quarantined for a few weeks, together with Idi in a private room in a hospital. The second time I was ten and stayed at home with Idi while the rest of the family was obliged to move out. I recall being visited by my school friends who stood on the sidewalk in front of the house while I leaned out the window to chat with them, feeling fine. When I was three I had a burst appendix, a very dangerous condition before the advent of antibiotics. I was rushed to the hospital and was operated on that night by Professor Lorenz, whom Mutti adored and referred to as '*eine Kapazität*' (expert), the highest praise she could bestow on anyone. She was a very doting and attentive mother, and Lesley recalls that when we were very young, she always dressed us in clothes from Bittmann's, Vienna's most prestigious children's store. When I was a little older, I appalled poor Mutti by my preference for wearing *Lederhosen*; I would give them the proper sheen by wiping my greasy fingers on them.

Playing soccer is what I enjoyed most. I followed the fortunes of Austria's vaunted "*Wunderteam*" (the first side from the continent to beat England) with enthusiasm, as did most Austrians. When a *Ländermatch* (international match) was being played, life almost came to a standstill in Vienna, as people on the street clustered around loudspeakers placed in front of shops (there was no TV). I was also devoted to my cub scout troop, and later to the Boy Scouts. The troop met once a week in a basement on the *Arenbergplatz* where we learned to tie different knots, to signal in Morse code, and by semaphore. Beside that, we always did a great deal of communal singing. We went on many day-excursions, and, occasionally, on longer camping trips. Amazingly, the Internet has made it possible for several of the surviving scouts to re-establish contact with each other. I visited one of them of them in Australia in 2000, and am in frequent email contact with another (Walter Wohlfeiler) who lives in Los Angeles. Whenever I am in Vienna, I always meet with a third (Martin Vogel). Wohlfeiler has sent me photographs and even a copy of our scoutmaster's log-book that let me re-live our hiking trips; particularly, an outing to the Schneeberg in 1936 when our *pathfinder* troop lost its way during the descent from the mountain, and we almost came to grief.

School held rather less fascination for me, but the close friendships I formed with classmates (Felix Weitzmann, Guido Colm) in high school were very important to me. They remain, to my regret, among the few close male friendships I have experienced. I attended the Volksschule (elementary school) for boys in the Strohgasse, just up the street from our house, for four years, but I remember only the emphasis placed on the development of calligraphic skills. These were then considered to be of paramount importance for one's future career (while today, it is being discussed whether cursive hand writing should be taught at all!). I am told that on the first day after vacation I ran up to my motherly teacher, Frau Uchatius, and gave her a kiss – it must have taken the lady aback. But my early school experience was hardly a happy one, for Lesley recalls that I was frequently nauseous and vomited before going to school.

It was on the Reisnerstrasse, on my way home from school when I was seven or eight, that I had my first encounter with anti-Semitism. I had got into some altercation with a kid in my class and when he called me a Saujud (Jew pig), I was at first astonished, and then knocked him down. This caused a big brouhaha and it came to the attention of the school principal who summoned Mutti to the school.

HIGH SCHOOL

When I was ten, I took the entrance examination to the *Akademisches Gymnasium*, a prestigious academic (Greek and Latin compulsory) high school founded in the 17th century and housed in a beautiful neo-Gothic building on the Beethoven Platz. I recall the excitement of going to the school on the appointed day in the spring and finding my name on the list of admitted students that was posted on the school's ornately carved front door. The school counts many illustrious names among its former students, among them Schubert, Hugo von Hoffmannsthal, the librettist of *Rosenkavalier*, as well as three renowned physicists, Ludwig Boltzmann, Lise Meitner, and Erwin Schrödinger. It was, like all schools of that era, segregated by sex, and it was not until my brief stay in a Canadian high school, many years later, that I had the strange and disconcerting experience of being in the same class with girls. The school is located next to a small park which is presided over by Beethoven's monument at its center. In winter, we boys fought spirited snowball battles from behind snow ramparts that we built in the park – under the scornful gaze of Beethoven seated on his pedestal.

The school work at the Gymnasium presented the first challenge for me, but I obtained reasonable grades in all subjects except in Latin – and proficiency in Latin was then still regarded as a measure of an educated person.[4] I place the blame for my poor performance in Latin squarely on my dreaded, irascible Latin teacher, Professor Lackenbacher, who remains indelibly engraved in my memory. When he chastised a pupil furiously as an *ignoramus* or worse, his face turned beet-red, and he played a leading role in my periodic nightmares. On one memorable occasion, however, when the star students in the class failed to answer a grammatical question he posed, I raised my hand and, mirabile dictu, came up with the correct answer. Whereupon Lackenbacher berated the entire class shouting: *"Sogar der Eisinger hat das gewußt!"* (Even Eisinger knew that!) That evening I related this incident, not without a little pride, to my parents, who were understandably uncertain how to regard it.

The study of Greek was compulsory in the third year at the Akademisches Gymnasium, and lacking faith in me as a classicist, my ever-practical mother transferred me to the Kaiser Franz Josef Realgymnasium (RG1) on the Stubenbastei, where the second required language was English, rather than Greek. Both schools were just a 15 minute walk through the Stadtpark from our home. In my new school, the Latin teacher was the kindly Professor Schläfrig under whom I fared much better. Though Professor Lackenbacher had initially made me despise Latin, I came to cherish the succinctness of the language in my more mature years and fifty years later, when I worked on the history of medicine, I was even able to put my high school-Latin to good use.

I generally brought a sandwich to school for lunch, but as a special treat, I could buy an *Einspänner* (hot dog) from the school janitor. In our physical education classes we did gymnastics and played *Völkerball* (dodge ball) in the schoolyard; but when it came to *Fußball* (soccer), the sport most boys loved best, we had to fend for ourselves. We usually played in parks or wherever we could find a reasonably level piece of ground, but for an all-important inter-class match we collected money from among our classmates and rented a proper soccer field in the *Prater*, Vienna's huge recreational park

School discipline was strict and formal. We addressed our teachers with *Herr* Professor – they were, of course, all men — and before each period, one student stood at the classroom door and when he saw the teacher approach, he shouted *Achtung!* whereupon we all stood at attention at our desks until the teacher had reached his desk on the podium in front, and told us to sit down. Tardiness, bad behavior, or missed homework would lead to your name being formally entered into the dreaded *Klassenbuch* and if the infraction was serious, your parent was summoned to the principal. This happened to me only once, when I was caught burning some paper inside my desk and the teacher noticed smoke curling out of the ink well. Mutti was called to a conference with the principal who gave her to understand that her son was likely to end up in a penitentiary.

My favorite subject was geography. I loved maps (I still do and have a collection of antique maps that go back to the 15th century) and I knew by heart the capital cities of all countries of the world. Our geography teacher, Professor Jasbetz, was a former army officer, as were many of our teachers, and when he took the class on an excursion in the Wienerwald, he had us solve problems in military tactics. We also played a war game for which we were divided into two armies, each guarding a fort and wearing a different colored strand of wool on the sleeve. If your strand was torn off by an 'enemy' you were 'dead' and out of the game.

My memory of what was taught in the different academic subjects is sketchy. Mathematics, Euclidean geometry and algebra, I had no trouble with, and the only bit of science that left an impression on me was a lecture-demonstration of liquefied air (really nitrogen) that a visiting physicist presented, as we sat on the floor of our gym. I could hardly have foreseen that many years later, I was to use copious amounts of liquid nitrogen and helium in my laboratory; or that I would present well-received liquid air demonstrations at the Village Community School when Alison and Simon were elementary school students there! In German composition classes we had to memorize many poems, mostly classics that everyone who attended school in Austria would retain, at least in snatches, for life. Composition exercises had to be written in the obsolescent German script (known as *Kurrent*), but we could use Latin script in all other subjects. Remarkably, I was able to put my familiarity with the German script to good use sixty years later, when I transcribed and translated hundreds of letters of Johannes Brahms for Styra's grand *opus Johannes Brahms. Life and Letters.* We also had classes in singing and drawing, which I enjoyed, and in religion, which I did not. For those classes, we were divided into Catholics, Jews, and *Konfessionslose* (those unaffiliated with any religion), whom I secretly envied, for I already had a skeptical attitude towards religious teachings.

I recall a class ski trip one winter when we stayed for several days in a dormitory in a *Kartause*, a former monastery, near Mariazell. Ski lifts were almost unknown then and we skied cross-country on wooden skis, climbing over fences when necessary. One afternoon we stopped off at a farmhouse where we had an afternoon snack (*Jause*) of bread and homemade *Presskopf* (headcheese). I can still recall its scrumptious peppery taste, partly because it was a forbidden fruit (always my favorite kind) and would not have passed muster even in our fairly relaxed kosher household (Mutti was known to enjoy a slice of ham, now and then). I recall similar skiing trips with my boy scout troop, when the younger cub scouts were subjected to very scary, but harmless, initiation rites by the older boys. In the evening, each new boy was blind-folded and was led into a room to be 'branded'. His arm was 'frozen' with snow and he heard sizzling as the branding iron branded him and he smelt flesh burning – albeit not his, but a piece of meat. It was all in fun. At all our weekly get-togethers, whether in our basement meeting room on the Arnbergplatz or around a camp fire, there was always a lot of singing. We all knew innumerable folk songs by heart, some dating from the Thirty Year War three centuries earlier, and some from the Spanish Civil War that was raging at the time. We scouts were all in sympathy with the Republicans in Spain who were fighting Franco and, indirectly, Hitler and Mussolini. Those songs form a curious bond among the surviving members of my Boy Scout troop with whom I am in touch (*Immer marschieren, immer verlieren; Wir sind die Moorsoldaten; Spiess voran, drauf und dran, setzt aufs Klosterdach den roten Hahn; etc*). Communal singing, generally, played a big part in social gatherings of young people in those days.

Our family's apartment was in the same building as that of the Kimmelmann family whose two children, Liesl and Hans, were the same age as Lesley and I. Lesley and Liesl were close friends (they still are), as were Hans and I. Feeling the need to be in constant communication, Hans and I constructed an aerial tramway that crossed the courtyard from the Kimmelmanns' fourth floor apartment to ours (Parterre) so that we could send messages to each other. I visited Liesl (now Elisabeth) in Melbourne two years ago (in 2000) and when I addressed her as 'Liesl', she winced noticeably for she had become thoroughly anglicized, as had her brother (now John Keeble by name), and both preferred not to be reminded of their roots. Their mother was a strikingly beautiful and elegant woman whose husband, Stefan Kimmelmann, had always taken a kindly interest in me. He will re-appear in a later chapter

SCENES FROM MY CHILDHOOD

On Sundays, when the weather was fair and I was not on a boy scout excursion, the family often went hiking in the Wienerwald, the wooded hills surrounding the city. Like many other Viennese, we took the *Elektrische* (tram) to its last stop, say, Grinzing, and hiked through the mostly deciduous woods to a meadow on the Kahlenberg. There we would have a picnic with the homemade fried chicken and potato salad that we brought along in our rucksack, and as a special treat Lesley and I were allowed to have a soft drink (known as a *Kracherl*). It came in a glass bottle sealed by porcelain cap fitted with rubber gasket, and when you opened it, it made a satisfying *scishshhhh* sound. On other Sundays the family took part in the ritualistic corso on the Ringstrasse, usually in the company of friends or family, ending up in the Stadtpark sitting on chairs and listening to the music which was provided by an orchestra in the ornate bandstand at Hübner's *Kursalon*. It played mostly Strauss and Lehar waltzes, but when they struck up Smetana's *El Moldava*, the Jews within earshot rose from their chairs and stood – for the melody also served as the Zionist anthem.

Papa was a bridge enthusiast and a strong player. Bridge was the preferred card game of the middle classes: ladies and children played rummy, while the working classes played *Tarock* and *Schnappseln*. On Saturday afternoons Papa left the shop in Mutti's capable hands and played bridge at the Meierei in the Stadtpark, a *Kaffeehaus* where a so-called *Bridge Dame* arranged compatible foursomes. I was allowed to kibitz on condition of keeping as still as a mouse. The play was for money, but the stakes were modest. Papa also liked playing Tarock, a game that was popular in the Austro-Hungarian army. It was customary to play a card by smacking it down on the table, accompanied with a fitting spirited exclamation. I still have an image of Papa and his favorite brother Johann playing Tarock with jocular bravado.

In the winter, after school, Lesley and I often went skating at the nearby *Wiener Eislaufverein*. That venerable institution still exists but the expanse of the (artificial) ice is greatly reduced since the Vienna Intercontinental Hotel now occupies much of the original site. A live orchestra in the raised band stand played waltzes to skate by, and on special occasions (*Fasching*), all skaters were required to appear in costume. Costume parties were in any case very popular in Vienna, among grown-ups, as well, as children. (See the photo of Lesley and me on one such occasion.) The most important social occasion of my parents was the annual Kostler Ball, from which they did not return home till early morning, toting balloons and covered in confetti. The ball was a get-together of the many Viennese Jews whose ancestors came from Kostel and other nearby Moravian towns.[5] When I was very little, going to sleep on the night of the Kostler Ball with my parents away was very unsettling and I recall overcoming my qualms by going to sleep in their bed and rushing to my own bed across the hall when I heard Papa's key in the front door.

Like most middle-class children, Lesley and I spent our summer holidays in the country, with our parents when we were very young, and later, without them. When I was three or four our family rented rooms at a farm *cum* inn (Oberer Eggl) in Prein-an-der-Rax, where we met the family of *Kapitän* Roth, about whom more in Appendix II. When we were older, we often spent the summer at our grandmother's (Omama) establishment in Skotschau, Poland; and one year (1934), with other relatives of my mother (the Kolbans) in Maribor, Slovenia – both towns had been part of Austria-Hungary not many years before. When I was about twelve I spent a summer at a children's camp on the Arzberg in Tyrol and spent another summer with Hans Kimmelmann and his beautiful mother Anni in a traditional farmhouse near Seefeld, then an insignificant village but now a mega-ski resort with high-rise hotels to accommodate tourists from nearby Germany. There, as in Skotschau, we children spent our days hiking, swimming, gathering mushrooms, or picking blueberries and blackberries in the mountains.

Sometime in the thirties Papa acquired a Fiat automobile, at a time when there still were few cars in the streets of Vienna[6]. He used it primarily for business trips to towns, big and small, in the Austrian provinces, for he always made it a point to call personally on his customers. I recall the rigorous exam he had to pass for his driver's license: you were expected to know how to drive and to shift gears, but also, how an internal combustion engine works and how to repair it when it breaks down. One summer, when I was about twelve, Papa took Idi and me on an extended business trip to Graz, Villach,

Salzburg, Innsbruck and other towns. I loved the drives in the Alps over the winding roads that were still largely unpaved and extremely dusty. Sometimes I accompanied Papa when he called on a customer's shop and I recall his expertise and the easy and cheerful manner he had with his customers. Few of his customers knew that Papa was Jewish. In 1937, before the Anschluss, when anti-Semitism was already rampant in Austria, one customer in a provincial town confided to Papa that he had heard that Papa's firm was Jewish, whereupon Papa assuaged his concern by assuring him that his firm was just as Jewish as he himself.

Occasionally, on a Sunday, the family piled into the Fiat and visited Papa's brother, Onkel Johann, and his sister, Tante Rosa, who lived in the small town of Zistersdorf, about 30 miles north of Vienna. Onkel Johann was a small-scale cattle dealer who bought and sold cows at town markets where he knew many of the farmers and often played Tarock with them in the local café. He owned a couple of fields outside the town and there was a small stable was attached to his modest one-story house in Zistersdorf, but I don't recall ever seeing more than one or two cows there. Once Onkel Johann and a farmer had struck a deal, they would seal it with a hand-shake and a *Stamperl* (jigger) of slivovitz (plum brandy) in a nearby café (see photo). Onkel Johann had a daughter, Frieda, and two sons, Oskar and Erich who worked with their father and played for the Zistersdorf Football Club, along with Erwin, the son of Tante Rosa.[7] On Sundays, when my three big cousins played, I was allowed to sit behind the goal (Erwin was the goalie) and retrieve balls that crossed the goal line. There are thrills for every age!

Erich and Erwin's devotion to football was to stand them in good stead. After the Anschluss, they were expelled from Zistersdorf, along with the town's other Jews. They tried to escape across the French border but were apprehended by a German border patrol. While they were being escorted to a police station they talked football with their captors, who had a change of heart and showed them a safe route across the border. From France they made their way to England and safety. Zistersdorf is in a wine-growing region, and Onkel Johann once took Papa and me into one of the deep wine cellars alongside a country road. There I was allowed to take part in sampling a few wines, but when I re-emerged into the bright sunshine, I almost passed out. That escapade with Papa, and the time when he drove the Fiat at the breakneck speed of 100 km/hr (60 mph) were kept from Mutti by a mutual understanding between father and son.

When Lesley and I spent the summer in Skotschau (Skoszowa), we stayed in the substantial building on the market square that was the home of the Lindner family and of its textile business. It had been founded by my great-great-great-grandfather Samson Lindner in 1820, as the sign over the shop proudly proclaimed. The square building at the corner of the town square (*Rynek*) had enclosed an interior courtyard with stables where horses and wagons used to be kept, but was now home to a flock of geese. Marischka, who had been in the family's employ forever, force-fed the geese every day, a dastardly practice intended to enlarge the animal's liver (*fois gras*) and one that distressed me deeply. The living quarters were on the second floor; a spacious glassed-in veranda ran along three sides of the interior courtyard walls. In the shop two long counters faced each other and behind them were shelves that reached up to the ceiling, piled high with bolts of cloth of every variety. The wooden floor of the shop was always kept covered with sawdust and was swept periodically, after it was sprinkled with water by use of a holed tin can swung from a string. Why the sawdust? On market days, the shop was crowded with customers, many of them Polish-speaking peasants who were barefoot and were in town to sell their produce and to buy cloth from which they made their own clothing.

Omama's home was also the home her son Siegfried (Onkel Friedl) and his family, but it was Omama who ruled the establishment with a firm hand. Not surprisingly, this often led to friction, particularly after Onkel Friedl married the beautiful, elegant, and liberated Tante Lizzi. Her daughter Hanni told me with some pride, that Lizzi had been the first woman in Skotschau to take up skiing. Omama, on the other hand, was very old-fashioned. A hairdresser came to the house to do her hair every morning, and it was a special concern of hers that her grandchildren acquire fine table manners.

In Skotschau Lesley and I were continually together with our three local girl cousins who were about the same age: Onkel Friedl's daughters, Hanni and Marianne, and Tante Alice's daughter, Hedi, who lived in nearby Bielitz (Bielsko). Together we hiked in the nearby mountains and swam in the Vistula river which flows through Skotschau. We teased each other mercilessly, and played practical jokes on our much-loved Tante Else, who never

23

complained of our gross sense of humor. Our three cousins spoke Polish, as well as German, and since they knew their way around, they were our guides in Skotschau and in the nearby towns where other Lindner relatives lived. I recall a visit to the saw mill in the foothills of the Carpathian Mountains that was owned by a relative, and particularly the thrill of riding down the mountainside on the narrow-gauge railway used to transport logs to the mill. Another relative of Mutti owned a leather tannery in Skotschau, and another owned the fragrant vinegar factory, and they were known, respectively, as the Leather-Spitzers and the Vinegar-Spitzers[8]. I fondly remember another relative, a lawyer in Bielitz, who presented me with my much-loved bicycle for my Bar Mitzvah.[9] It was mostly in Skotschau that I saw my somewhat older cousins, Gerti, Poldi, and Edith, even though they also lived in Vienna. Indeed, when I visited my cousin Edith Robinsohn (born in 1909) in Los Angeles in 2000, she commented that the last time she recalled seeing me, I was still wearing short pants. These three older cousins were often the subject of the dinner conversations at Omama's table, in which their elders scrutinized their liaisons with members of the opposite sex (added in 2016: Edith lived California until she died, aged 105).

My most memorable summer vacation was one that Mutti, Lesley and I spent together with the Boyko family in Lovrano, a town on the Adriatic that had already been a favorite summer resort in ancient Rome[10]. Hugo and Lisa Boyko were both academics (botanists), and close friends of my parents. Their three children (Eva, Maja, and Herbert) were about the same age as Lesley and I. We five spent a lot of time together, often at their grandmother's house and orchard in Ober St. Veidt, a suburb of Vienna, where we picked berries and apricots that we brought home to Idi who preserved them as jam or compote for consumption in winter. The Boykos were devoted Zionists and emigrated to Palestine well before the *Anschluss*. Both had successful research careers in Israel where they worked on the cultivation of commercially useful, salt-tolerant plants.

Lovrana evokes memories of train travel in the 1930s. Air conditioning did not exist, and in summer the windows in the carriages were kept open, not without repeated warnings from our parents not to lean out because cinders from the coal-fired locomotive would get into your eyes. The windows had to be closed quickly when the train approached a tunnel, otherwise the compartment would fill with smoke and soot. It was in Lovrano that I beheld the sea for the first time, an experience that left a deep impression on me. I confess to being susceptible to the call of the sea, still. Some seemingly trivial incidents of that summer remain engraved in my mind, such as riding in a water taxi along the coast and hearing the captain shout: *'Avanti! Avanti!* each time the little cutter departed from a landing—*Avanti! Avanti!* Another very clear memory is of the walk along the shore of the Adriatic on which I had my first taste of fresh figs; I still recall the occasion whenever fresh figs now come my way.

On the return journey from sunny Italy to Vienna, our little party stopped for a few days at an inn in the Austrian Alps, and the contrast could not have been greater: A steady rain turned the village road to mud, and it was so cold that we five children stayed in bed under huge feather beds all day and amused ourselves with endless word games. However did we get along so happily without television, the internet, DVDs, or mobile telephones!

* * *

These paragraphs reflect my jumbled recollections of life in pre-*Anschluss* Vienna. While writing them, it occurred to me that the urban, middle-class life I took for granted in my childhood was very different from the small town settings in which both my parents had grown up, Papa in Moravia and Mutti in Upper Silesia (Oberschlesien). Following the gradual emancipation of Jews beginning in the 18th century, Vienna became a magnet for many Jews from these regions. For the first time in many centuries Jews were free to travel, to own property, to reside wherever they pleased, and to practice professions that had long been closed to them. The energy with which the more enterprising among them pursued the new opportunities had much in common with that of immigrants arriving in America, another Land of Opportunity, at the end of the 19th century.

My parents could hardly have foreseen that after having successfully built their lives in Vienna, they would have to make two more fresh starts later, first in Israel. and again, in Canada. But thanks to the survival skills that were their heritage, they succeeded. I hope that my children have retained the skills needed for flourishing in ever-changing, and often hostile environments.

NOTES

[1]His most ambitious invention was a rotary internal combustion engine. After the Anschluss he had me deliver blueprints of the engine to the French Legation in Vienna in hopes of arousing sufficient interest that might lead to a visa.

[2]In spite of the bitter resentment he harbored against Mathilde, he always took care of his neurotic sister. When Lesley and I were children, Tante Mathilde came to our flat every week for a bath. Her visits were scary for she was somewhat paranoid and easily got mad at us if we teased or contradicted her. When she was young she had gone to the US together with her sister Hanni and they had done well there, but their mother, Anna, insisted that they return to Kostel to marry. Grandmother Anna was blamed for saddling them with unsuitable husbands, although that may have been related to their modest dowries: Hanni was married to a hunchback and Mathilde to a rogue who abandoned her soon after fathering a daughter, Fritzi Tannenblatt. Both Mathilde and Hanni died in the Holocaust, but Fritzi survived and her grandson, Martin Gewing, lives in Los Angeles.

[3]We were often content with a ball game we called *"Köpfeln"* in the Stadtpark. Two pairs of trees facing each other served as the goals and you tried to head the ball into your opponent's goal while standing in your own. You could make a stop with hands or feet, but if you did so with your head, you were entitled to take a free header from halfway between the goals.

[4]I visited the Akademisches Gymnasium in May 2008 and was accorded an extremely friendly welcome by the teachers. The school had undergone momentous changes since I had been a student, the most noticeable being that half the students and almost all teachers are women. The teachers kindly sent me transcripts of my grades from 1934-36 which show what an undistinguished student I was. I received 'sufficient' grades in History, Science, Geography and Mathematics and my 'insufficient' in Latin had obliged me to pass special exams at the end of the summer vacation before being allowed to enter the next grade. I received 'good' grades in Drawing, German, Physical Education, and Schriftpflege (handwriting) and earned my only 'very good' grade in Singing.
Styra and I visited the school again in May 2009 and attended a commemoration marking the expulsion of Jewish students in 1938. It was a moving affair, held in the school's ornate Festsaal and I was astonished to learn that each year, three classes of the school traveled to Auschwitz and reported on the experience upon their return.

[5]I always suspected that Kostel's name derived from a Roman castellum on its site. Styra, Alison and Simon presented me in 2001 with the new and glorious 'Barrington Atlas of the Greek and Roman World' for Father's Day, and sure enough, it shows Kostel/Podivin as a Roman settlement between 30 BCE and 300 ACE. As a boy in Vienna I was keenly aware of Vienna being the heir of Roman Vindobona: To this day the usual greeting between friends in Vienna is the Latin *Servus* (your servant) and an inscription on war ministry sported the inscription: *DULCE DECORUM PRO PATRIA MORI (It is sweet and proper to die for the fatherland -- Cicero's sentiment).*

[6]Our building had central steam heat, but hot water was not provided and the bathwater was heated in

a cylindrical gas water heater. There was a laundry room in the basement, but there were no washing machines, refrigerators, or freezers, but we did have an ice box. In the hall just before you reached the kitchen there was a wall telephone – the number was B 55 6 16 – with a little dial that kept track of your usage. Long-distance calls were very expensive and had to be ordered in advance.

[7]Tante Rosa and her husband Leopold Maas ran a small haberdashery shop in Zistersdorf. They, Onkel Johann and his wife, also named Rosa, all perished in the Holocaust (but all five of their children survived). After they were evicted from Zistersdorf, they had moved to Vienna. I have translated Onkel Johann's heart-breaking letters to Frieda written in Vienna as the conditions for Jews worsened. Eventually Onkel Johann and his ailing wife Rosa were deported 'to the East' and were shot to death in Maly Trostinec, near Kiev, on 11 May 1942.

In 2000 I visited Melbourne, Australia, to help celebrate my cousin Frieda Redlich's ninetieth birthday there, and am again in touch with her sons Max, who ran his father's butcher shop, and Peter, who became an eminent labor lawyer (now deceased). They and Oskar's children, also Australians, have sired numerous descendents with the most varied lifestyles, including a Buddhist priest and an orthodox Lubovicher. Erich chose to return to England, at least partly because of the higher standard of football there and his daughter and grandchildren live in Spain. Strange to say, most of the descendents of Kostel's Josef Rüderer Eisinger are now Australians! What's more, I just heard from another great grandson of Josef Rüderer's brother Ignatz, who lives in Perth, Australia, about as far away from Austria as one can get. His name is Robert Fraser (2004).

[8]The last owner of the tannery was Oscar Spitzer, whose daughter Monica Strauss is my closest, dearly beloved 'rellie' in New York. In 2002 she joined Styra and me in exploring Sicily.

Sad to say, Omama, Hedi and her mother Alice perished in Auschwitz. When the Germans invaded Poland in 1939, Onkel Friedl urged Omama, his mother, strenuously to join him and his family and flee to the East, but she insisted on staying in the house in which she was born and had lived in her entire life, saying 'After all, what can they do to an old lady?' (Was können sie schon einer alten Frau antun?)

[9]In 1937 I had my bar mitzvah in Vienna's oldest synagogue, the Seitenstetten Tempel, and my chanting of the Thora section earned high praises from both the rabbi and my father!

[10]The town, known to the ancient Romans as Lauriana, was in Austria-Hungary until 1918, and it was in Italy when I visited it as a boy. It had become part of Yugoslavia when Simon and I were there in 1983, and it is now in Croatia.

My debut,
1924.

Dressed up for a
costume party,
ca. 1930.

With my big sister and all dolled up, ca. 1927.

Lesley with Mutti

...and with cousin Marianne,
Skotschau 1934.

My class in the Akademische Gymnasium on an excursion in the Vienna Woods, 1935. I am in the rear, wearing lederhosen and a tie. Jasbetz (Geography) and Grossmann (Drawing) are the teachers on the right.

My boy scout troop on an hiking trip to the Rax mountain. I am in the rear, second from right, ca. 1934.

A Jause at Onkel Johann's home to celebrate the engagement of cousin Hilda and Erwin Zweigenthal. Papa is 3rd from left with Onkel Johann on his left. Cousins Erwin, Erich and Oskar are standing in the rear.

The photo records the sale of a cow and its calf. Onkel Johann, far right, is seen slapping hands with a farmer who bought/sold the pair. Zistersdorf, ca. 1910.

This postcard documents Skotschau's ceremonial incorporation into Poland following the First World War. Far left: The Lindner homestead on the market square with family members watching from the windows.

The sign over the shop reads: SAMSON LINDNER, Founded 1820.

Omama Lindner and cousins Hanni, Gerti and Marianne. Skotschau, ca. 1929.

Papa and Mutti in their bedroom in the Reisnerstrasse, reading a card from Lesley in England. The tile stove behind them was never used because the house had central steam heat. 1939.

2

FLIGHT TO ENGLAND

ANSCHLUSS

On March 12, 1938, one day before a plebiscite to decide Austria's independence and political future was to take place, Hitler's army occupied Austria without meeting any resistance, even as Austria's prime minister Schuschnigg, choking back tears, resigned in a radio address. The days leading up to that momentous event had been filled with passionate propaganda from both sides of the plebiscite issue and in that age before television, that meant that countless posters and graffiti covered building walls and thousands of leaflets littered the city streets. The Nazis called for union with Germany while the slogan of Austria's ruling party, the *Vaterländische Front*, championed the country's continued independence with the oft-chanted slogan, *rot-weiß-rot bis in den Tod* (red–white–red unto death). Although that party had fascistic roots of its own, having waged a short civil war against the social-democratic opposition in 1934, public sentiment seemed to be leaning in favor of independence, when Hitler's invasion made the issue moot and, incidentally, changed the tranquil course of my own life profoundly.

In Vienna, palpable change was not long in coming. German warplanes flew low over the city and all over town, German soldiers in half-track personnel carriers rolled through the streets while military bands played marches in many squares of the city. To eliminate any conceivable opposition, tens of thousands of Austrians who had criticized the Nazis or had been politically active – be they socialists, monarchists, unionists, artists, writers, journalists – were arrested within days of the *Anschluss*, using arrest lists that had been prepared for years beforehand. Frightful stories soon began to leak out of the Dachau and Buchenwald concentration camps, and the brutality exhibited by local Nazi thugs in the streets, principally directed against Jews, was overt. It was quickly revealed that many Austrians had been *Illegale*, i.e. had been clandestine members of the Nazi party, which had been outlawed since its failed *Putsch* in 1934 when Nazis murdered the Austrian Chancellor Engelbert Dollfuss in his office. Some of my teachers were among the "illegals" who were readily identifiable by the distinctive insignia of the Nazi Party (NSDAP) that they sported in their lapels. Everyone quickly understood that these insignias carried incomparably greater weight than the plain swastikas that were soon worn by almost everyone. Jews were forbidden to do so, even if they had been so inclined, and this rendered them vulnerable, long before they were forced to wear the yellow star some three years later. Being young and foolish, I would occasionally stick a swastika pin in my lapel so I could go to the opera or the cinema - an act of bravura strongly disapproved of by my parents. Under the Nazis, I learned making myself inconspicuous in public – and I never got over it.

It is not my purpose to offer an historical account of what transpired following the *Anschluss*, the incorporation of Austria into Germany. I will briefly sketch the political scene and will confine myself to my own experiences in Nazi-occupied Vienna. These were, fortunately, quite innocuous compared to the fate of the thousands of Austrian Jews who were imprisoned, deported and murdered in the subsequent years.[1]

Excitement gripped many, though by no means all, Viennese and huge crowds welcomed Hitler and the German troops jubilantly. I witnessed such a scene on the Ringstrasse where a crowd had assembled in front of the hotel where Hitler was staying. They chanted: *Nach Hause, nach Hause, nach Hause gehn wir nicht, bis dass der Führer spricht, . . .!* (We won't go home until the Führer speaks). Hitler duly appeared on the balcony and languidly raised his arm in the Nazi salute to his adoring public. Within days wooden display cases appeared on the walls of many buildings that displayed copies of the *Völkischer Beobachter*, the official newspaper that offered Göbbels' version of the news, along with Streicher's infamous anti-Semitic newspaper

Der Stürmer whose vicious lies about Jews were particularly infuriating to me. Grotesque caricatures of Jews were a specialty of the paper, clearly intended to dehumanize Jews. In Austria, where wide-spread anti-Semitism had long been tolerated, if not espoused, by the Catholic Church, such propaganda fell on receptive ears. I recall seeing the proclamation by Vienna's Cardinal Innitzer posted on a billboard on my block, which urged Vienna's citizens to support the Führer and his government. His honeymoon with Hitler was short-lived: when Innitzer showed some independence a few weeks later, his palace was smashed by Nazis. Columns of the *Hitler Jugend* (Hitler Youth) and SA men in their brown uniforms marched in the streets, singing Nazi songs, the Horst Wessel Lied and 'When Jewish blood spurts from the knife, things go twice as well' (*Wenns Judenblut vom Messer spritzt . . .*) Among Jews and political opponents of the Nazis (Vienna had a socialist past and was known as 'Red Vienna') there was fear and shock. It was a favorite sport of Nazis to force Jews, old and young, to scrub the sidewalks with toothbrushes, surrounded by a jeering mob. On one occasion I witnessed a German army officer who saw such a pathetic scene, actually berating the Viennese bystanders!

The efficiency of the Nazis was remarkable. Within a few days of the *Anschluss*, two members of the *Hitler Jugend* showed up at our apartment and demanded my khaki Boy Scout shirt, presumably to alleviate the shortage in brown shirts caused by recent events. The Boy Scouts were outlawed and disbanded, along with all other clubs and organizations not affiliated with the Nazi Party. My school, the *Realgymnasium* on the Stubenbastei, was closed and German troops were quartered there for several weeks. When it re-opened, all Jewish students were expelled and were transferred to an all-Jewish gymnasium in the Sperlgasse in Vienna's 2nd District, but before long that school was closed down, as well.

But school attendance was soon among the lesser concerns of Viennese Jews: Their ability to earn a living was proscribed more and more severely, they were evicted from public housing and forbidden to enter public parks, cinemas or theaters. Their persecution reached a climax on 9 November 1938, cynically referred to as *Reichskristallnacht*, 'National Night of Broken Glass'. On that day most synagogues were smashed or burnt in Germany, which now included Austria, and many Jews were arrested and shipped to the Dachau or Buchenwald concentration camps. My immediate family was relatively fortunate:

37

Two SA men appeared in the shop on the Hoher Markt and unceremoniously robbed Papa of his shop and business. They did not arrest him, possibly because he showed them the medal for bravery he had earned in WWI that he wore under his coat. They simply demanded his keys and rudely told him to get lost (*Shauns daß Sie weiterkommen!*). Many other Jewish men were not so lucky.

We were good friends of the Diamant family whose son Hans, a medical student, had at one time tutored me in Latin and was one of Lesley's first boyfriends. Ironically, their other son, Bobby, was still in the Austrian army that was now incorporated into the *Wehrmacht*. On *Kristallnacht* their father, a physician, had been warned that he would be arrested if he returned to their apartment, and so the whole family moved in with us.[2] Their apartment was located in the Leopoldstadt (Vienna's 2nd District) where many Jews lived and where the ferocity of the Nazis was unrestrained. We were fortunate to live in Vienna's 3rd District in a neighborhood that housed many foreign diplomatic missions and where the Nazis were at pains to cultivate a civilized image.[3]

Deep gloom now descended upon the Jews of Vienna, their irrepressible gallows humor and whispered Hitler jokes notwithstanding. They bent all their efforts to finding a way out of 'Greater Germany' and their efforts grew more urgent following the annexation of Czechoslovakia in March 1939. But it was easier to accept the concept of emigration than to put it into practice, for there were few countries that were willing to accept Jews without imposing insurmountable financial conditions. Papa wrote to a business acquaintance in England who had supplied him with chamois leather in former days, and described his and his family's vanishing prospects in Vienna. That gentleman passed Papa's letter on to a friend, a Sephardic Jew, H.G. de Costa by name, who agreed to provide the guarantee that enabled Lesley, then seventeen, to obtain a visa for England and to work as an *au-pair* girl in the de Costa's home. In the autumn of 1938 she was the first of our immediate family to escape, and I well remember the excitement with which we read her letters after she arrived in London.

Scores of rumors about potential escape routes made the rounds among the Viennese Jews. The lucky ones had relatives in the USA and were eligible for affidavits which entitled them to apply for a visa, others made it to Shanghai, the only destination on this Earth that - for a time – required no landing permits or visas.[4]   A handful of countries did admit Jewish refugees with saleable skills, and popular wisdom among the Viennese Jews had it, that knowing a useful trade greatly improved one's chance of obtaining an immigration visa. This gave rise to an *Umschulung* (re-schooling) industry for teaching trades that were deemed to be in demand. Thus, Papa enrolled in a watch-making course and earned an ornate diploma attesting to his newly acquired skill, while I took two such courses: one qualified me to work as an electrician, and the other, of all things, as a blacksmith! That course was taught by the Jewish blacksmith from Zistersdorf who had been expelled from that town, along with the Eisingers and the other Jews who lived there.

Since Jews were now forbidden to listen to foreign radio broadcasts or to own radios, we presented our lovely new radio to our janitor, a decent man who invited us to listen to the news in his apartment. He also kept roaming thugs from our building by telling them that it housed no Jewish tenants (there were two families). Money became increasingly tight and I was lucky to land a part-time job delivering pastries from a bakery to patisseries (*Konditorei*) and cafés all over the city. I used my bicycle and strapped on my back was a pack board holding cardboard boxes of pastries, such as *Kremschnitten* and *Punschkrapfen*. It was no mean trick to keep the pastry boxes level while pedaling through traffic, on cobble-stoned streets laced with streetcar tracks: keeping the front wheel of the bike from slipping into a streetcar track was a constant concern.

In their all-consuming quest for visas, passports and the other documents needed by would-be emigrants, aspirants waited in long queues in front of consulates and government offices. These queues often formed in the evening before the day when the office opened for business. I particularly recall the many hours it took to procure the infamous *Steuerliche Unbedenklichkeitsbescheinigung*, the document that certified that you owed no taxes. The queues were favorite targets of police and of Nazi thugs, out for a night of harassing or arresting Jews. Since it was considered less likely for a boy to be arrested than an adult, it often fell to me to get up at midnight or in the early morning hours in order to hold a place in a queue for a relative. When I am now obliged to get up in the dark of night, it reminds me of how I felt when I was woken up to get dressed and to join some dismal queue.

Until 1940, it was the Nazis' policy to 'cleanse' Vienna of its Jews by depriving them of their livelihood, arresting men and frightening them into emigration. Later, their policy changed to deporting all Jews to the East where virtually all were murdered. But before the policy of extermination was put into effect, there existed a bizarre escape route from Vienna that is not widely known. It was facilitated by the unlikely alliance between William Perl, a young Viennese Jewish attorney, and Adolf Eichmann, the Nazi official charged with ridding Vienna of its Jews.

After the *Anschluss*, Perl, a dedicated Zionist, was arrested and was being interrogated by Eichmann when he told his tormentor that he could transport large numbers of Jews from Vienna to Palestine if permitted to do so. His plan was to charter river steamers to take the refugees down the Danube to a river port near the Black Sea, there to board sea-going ships that would take the refugees to the coast of Palestine where the refugees would scramble ashore. Since the British were at that time enforcing a strict embargo on Jewish immigration in order to gain Arab support in the war, the scheme Perl proposed would not only get Jews out of Vienna, but would at the same time, tweak the tail of the British lion. Astonishingly, the plan appealed to Eichmann and with his co-operation and funds raised abroad it was eventually realized.

Although the ships used in these 'illegal transports' were dreadfully over-crowded and under-provisioned, and were constantly harassed by Nazis, some forty thousand Jews managed to reach Palestine, although many others were shipwrecked or fell into Nazi hands. This is the perilous route by which my parents escaped from Vienna, and it is described more fully in Appendix II.[5]

In the period between the *Anschluss* and the beginning of WWII, Adolf Eichmann sanctioned another scheme to reduce the number of Jews in Vienna: transporting Jewish children from Germany, Austria and Czechoslovakia by train to any country willing to accept them. These so-called *Kindertransports* had been proposed to Eichmann by a remarkably courageous Dutch woman, Gertrud Wijsmuller-Meijer. After suffering many indignities and arrest, her scheme succeeded in saving the lives of thousands of children. To the best of my knowledge, England was the only country willing to accept these children and it was by means of such a *Kindertransport* that I made my escape from Vienna in April 1939.[6]

I can only surmise how my name found its way onto a *Kindertransport* list of children scheduled to leave for England. Each child had to be sponsored either by an organization or an individual, and it is likely that Mr. de Costa had lent his name as my sponsor. Each child was allowed to take one small suitcase, and I recall lengthy discussions regarding the selection of items that would be most useful to me in the Great Unknown. Papa's riding boots from World War I were among them, as was a wooden 'mushroom' used for darning holes in socks, and I was indeed to make use of both of these items. The emphasis on darning socks sounds strange today, but before the invention of synthetic fibers the heels and toes of socks were forever wearing out. Mutti gave me a refresher course in darning socks, sewing on buttons and doing laundry by hand, and I practiced what was considered to be of paramount importance in England: how to use knife and fork in the English (and seemingly irrational) manner, i.e. with the tines of the fork pointing down!

When the day of my departure arrived, Mutti accompanied me to the railway station, the *Westbahnhof*. I wore my tweed knickerbockers, the usual attire of Viennese teenager (I had just turned fifteen), an outfit that prompted people in England to ask if I was on my way to play golf. The station was crawling with police and Gestapo men, who searched our suitcases for money and other contraband. They taunted the unhappy parents and forbade them to display any emotion or distress while saying good-bye on the platform--on pain of the transport being cancelled. After we children had boarded the railway carriages, a Nazi official found it amusing to have us sing a folksong familiar to every Austrian child as the train pulled out of the station: *"Muss I denn, muss I denn zum Städtle hinaus und du mein Schatz bleibst hier . ."* (Must I, oh must I leave this town while you, my dear one, stays here ...)

Many years later, Mutti told me that after she returned home, distraught and uncertain if she would ever see me again, she described the appalling scene at the station to Idi, who was almost a member of our family and had lived with us since Lesley was born. Yet Idi was not immune to Nazi propaganda and when Mutti finished, Idi exclaimed: "If the *Führer* only knew of this, he would surely put a stop to it!"[7]

SAFE HAVEN IN ENGLAND

For a boy growing up in Vienna, England had the aura of a distant, exotic country in those days. The excitement of the unknown adventures that lay ahead tempered my distress at leaving my home and country. All I can recall of the journey is looking out the window of our sealed carriage and watching the familiar Alpine landscape fade into the novel and flat countryside of Holland. In Hoek van Holland our train was shunted onto a railway ferry and we crossed the Channel still ensconced in our carriages. When we finally arrived at London's Victoria Station, nametags were hung around our necks and as we sat on wooden benches in a cavernous waiting room, our names were called out, one by one. As each nervous child was summoned to the table manned by committee officials, it picked up its suitcase and was introduced to its English sponsor. The hall had almost been emptied when an official came to me and told me that since no sponsor had come forward to claim me, I would have to be sent back to Germany.

While I was sitting by myself on a bench digesting this dismal piece of news and keeping an eye on my suitcase, a young man approached and sat down beside me. Quietly he told me (in English!) that his name was Alec and that he was Mr. de Costa's son. He then had me point out my suitcase, checked his watch, and indicating a door on the far right side of the hall, he told me quietly: "When I say: 'Now, Joey', I will pick up your suitcase and we will both make a dash for that door on the right." He kept an eye on his watch and when he gave the signal, we both sprinted to the indicated door which was unlocked and opened onto a narrow driveway. At the same moment, a car pulled up, Alec opened the rear door, and we jumped in, even as the car with Mr. de Costa at the wheel, sped off – pursued by a group of gesticulating officials.

Apparently, Mr. de Costa had either changed his mind or had never intended to sponsor me. Having declined to sign the requisite sponsorship documents, even after being told that I would have to be returned to Germany, he and Alec had taken matters in their own hand and had concocted their meticulously synchronized kidnapping scheme – and executed it flawlessly.

They took me to the de Costas' apartment located on 5 Hyde Park Corners, near Marble Arch, and there Lesley and I had a joyous reunion. This was my only visit to Mr. de Costa's home and he made it clear to me that he had done all he planned to do for me. I thanked him for having abducted me and told him that I felt nothing but gratitude towards him. He was by profession a tipster, a person who offers tips on horse races to his clients and in return, earns a commission if, and only if, the horse he touted was a winner. In this perfectly legal enterprise he relied on good inside information which he obtained from jockeys of his acquaintance. This explained Lesley's puzzling observation that so many of Mr. de Costa's visitors were men of unusually small stature!

This is how it came about that I began my new life in England as an illegal alien. But that did not diminish my delight at find myself in the strange and wondrous city of London, so different from Vienna. Here people put milk in their tea, instead of lemon, rode in double-decker buses that drove on the wrong (left) side of the street, and traveled in underground trains with upholstered seats instead of wooden benches!

Alec de Costa was then eighteen years old and was an aspiring organ builder. Alas, he developed a romantic interest in Lesley, and since his mother was not thrilled by her only son marrying a penniless refugee girl, she fired Lesley, who was obliged to find work elsewhere. When a few months after I arrived in London, Hitler invaded Poland and began WWII, Alec joined the RAF and became a Spitfire pilot during the Battle of Britain. Stationed in a small town in Scotland, he became involved with a local girl and when she became pregnant, he married her, and after the war, they settled there. He was still living there when sixty years later (2000), Lesley's daughter Debbie Ferguson spent a sabbatical year as a teacher in Britain. She tracked down Alec's address, Lesley traveled to Scotland, and they had a re-union – sixty years after they had parted.

For a few weeks after arriving in London, I slept on sofas in the flats of friends and relatives, all members of the growing refugee communities in Golders Green and Hampstead. I spent my days exploring London, going to the cinema, and occasionally having tea amid the opulence of Lyon's Corner House. I called on the various refugee organizations for guidance every day, but my murky legal status made them reluctant to deal with my case. Eventually, a place was found for me at the Stoatley Rough School, an agricultural training school in Haslemere, Surrey, where I was to earn my keep as a handyman. Potatoes were the staple food at the school and one of my daily chores was peeling several buckets of them with a knife – the potato peeler had not yet been invented! I also performed pick-and-shovel work excavating a swimming pool and became adept at navigating a wheelbarrow, fully loaded with dirt, up the steeply sloping planks from the excavation site. I was supervised by a tough foreman, a Jewish refugee from Prussia, who brooked no idleness. It was my first introduction to hard manual labor.

I ate my meals together with the students in the school dining room, but I did not attend any of their classes. Breakfast consisted of porridge every day, except on Sundays, when we were treated to corn flakes and each of us received one slice of canned pineapple – all new foods for me. One day I was summoned to the school office and was told that a permanent position had been found for me. I was to be a 'lad' (rhymes with 'mud') at the Low Farm in Bishop Monkton, Yorkshire, and I was to leave for there immediately.

LIFE AT THE LOW FARM

Bishop Monkton is an ancient village between Ripon and Harrogate which was recorded as "Monucheton" (Monks' town) in William the Conqueror's Doomsday Book (1086). The village was geographically, as well as in societal sense, a long way from the sheltering refugee community in London. It was also a long way from the urban life I had grown up with and had always taken for granted. Although I was getting used to speaking and understanding English, I found the Yorkshire dialect and the ways of my employers very strange and unsettling at first. It took me a long time before I could fit myself into their world, a world that retained many vestiges of the feudal past. To cushion my isolation I bought a notebook with black cardboard covers at Woolworth's in Ripon, the nearest town, and began keeping a diary, to which I confided my situation and my uncertain feelings over the next several years.

The Low Farm was operated by the Morland family who lived in a brick farmhouse on Boroughbridge Road, within walking distance from the village proper. The Morlands had for a long time rented the farm from the local 'gentleman' (squire), a certain Captain Fox, who apparently owned most of the land around Bishop Monkton. He lived in an impressive house with a tennis court at the edge of the village and I was to have a bizarre encounter with him later on.

The senior Mr. Morland seemed to me as a mean and sullen old man, too fragile to work in the fields, but continuing to run the farm with an iron hand. Every morning he assigned the day's chores to me and to his two sons, Tom and Kenneth, who seemed to have as little love for him, as I. I did not care much for Mrs. Morland either, for she liked to order me about. On Saturday afternoons which were supposedly my "time off" until milking time, she had me sweep the cobble-stoned front yard and whitewash the stonework and steps of the farm house, instead. Finally, there was the Morlands' marriageable daughter Ada who did the cooking, fed the geese and chickens, and gathered their eggs from hiding places all over the old stone barn. Reading and writing did not come easily to the Morlands and they called on me to read and write their occasional letters.

When I first arrived at the Low Farm, I was asked many questions about London, its tall buildings and the Underground, for no-one from Bishop Monkton had ever been to London, apart from the postmaster, who also kept the only shop of the village. Tom Morland was older and more serious-minded than Kenneth, who was then about twenty and was to become a noted cricketer for Yorkshire. But he got his start with the Bishop Monkton Cricket Club which played on Sundays on the meadow next to the farm house – but only after Ken and I had collected all the cow pats on the morning of a match, for on weekdays, the cricket pitch served as a pasture. Eventually Tom, Ken, and Ada all got married and settled on nearby farms. In 2001 Ken's widow, Margaret was the only member of that generation still living. After marrying Ken, she lived with him on the Low Farm where her relationship with her mother-in-law, Mrs. Morland, was as disagreeable as mine had been – and that formed a special bond between us. Styra, our two kids and I have visited Margaret twice in her little house in Bishop Monkton, and she confided to us that she says a prayer for us every evening. This reminded me of Niels Bohr who while visiting a student had asked him about the horseshoe mounted over his front door, whether he thought it brought him luck: "Of course, I don't believe in it, but it seems to work, anyway!"

The 'front room' was by far the most important room in the farmhouse, the only room heated by a fireplace and the only room with electric light – telephones had not reached the Low Farm. The front room also served as the kitchen where all the cooking was done in the coal-fed fireplace and it also served as the family dining room. Since it contained a stone sink with a manual pump, it also served as the washroom for the family. I say for the family, for as a mere lad, I was told to wash in a nearby small brick outbuilding which was also equipped with a pump and stone sink, and was otherwise used for slaughtering pigs. I slept in the unheated garret, directly above the front room, where the temperature fell to below freezing in the winter. The farmhouse did have a well-furnished parlor, but to the best of my recollection, it was only used once a year: on Boxing Day, when families from the neighboring farms called on the Morlands on their visiting rounds, and were served the traditional offerings of cheese and wine in the parlor.

At harvest time and at haying time, we worked particularly hard, from before dawn until after dark, when the usual chores and the milking had to be done. Instead of returning to the farmhouse at mid-day, Ada would bring lunch out to the field where we worked and we would eat it sitting under a tree. Yorkshire pudding was often on the menu, sometimes two or three times a day, and Mrs. Morland took special pride in her superior, secret recipe – as did all the other women in the village. We ate Yorkshire pudding not only with the Sunday roast, but also with soup, and sometimes, as dessert, smothered in treacle, a sticky sugar syrup that is popular in England. The remains of the Sunday roast underwent several metamorphoses during the remainder of the week and finally ended up as Shepherd's Pie. But we also ate a lot of mutton, which had a different taste from today's lamb, or rabbit stew whenever Tom had been successful with the shotgun. Rabbits were hunted by blocking all but one of a warren's entrances and letting a tethered ferret chase out the rabbits. Keeping ferrets was, however, not without its perils, for when one of the critters escaped from its cage one night, it got into a henhouse and murdered its entire population.

In 1995 I visited the Low Farm again, with my family, 55 years after I had left. The farmhouse had been thoroughly modernized and was now occupied by the family of a businessman who commuted to his office in Leeds every day. The house, along with the ancient stone barn, the stables, stone sheds and the barnyard were no longer attached to the fields and pastures surrounding them and these now empty farm buildings stood forlorn and without purpose. The former barnyard was still bordered by the ancient cobble-stone walkway and the stables, but the central area which used to be knee-deep in manure mixed with straw, now sported a neatly trimmed and understandably lush lawn. It was a sunny summer day and I was not easily able to visualize that this was where I used to fork manure into a cart before spreading it in the fields. That had been my favorite chore in winter because the manure generated enough heat to thaw out my freezing toes inside my Wellingtons.

The world has changed so profoundly since I was a lad in Yorkshire, a few reminiscences of life on the Low Farm may be of interest. The farm, typical of others scattered around Bishop Monkton, consisted of over a dozen fields and pastures, not all contiguous and totaling 130 acres. We grew a bewildering variety of crops and kept a full complement of livestock, including geese and chickens, pigs, a hundred sheep, a dozen cows and half a dozen draft horses. Crops of wheat, oats, barley, potatoes, turnips, and hay were rotated every year in fields that were bordered by hedge rows and connected by dirt lanes running between hedge rows. The turnips and hay were not sold, but stored as fodder for the livestock during the winter. Only one farmer in the village, our neighbor, owned a tractor and he was the butt of many jokes when his tractor got mired in the ever-present mud and had to be pulled out by our horses. When ploughing you held on to the handles of a single-blade plough drawn by a single horse, while also holding on to the reins. Harrowing was done in much the same way, but the horse-drawn hay rake used at haying time, one could sit on; even the rented 'self-binder' which cut the wheat and bundled it into sheaves at harvest time, was horse-drawn. Hay, turnips, and the other crops were hauled in two-wheeled wooden carts hitched to a single draft horse, a design that has changed little since classical antiquity. For hauling hay or sheaves the cart was fitted with a wooden frame which created a platform for the enormous loads of hay we piled onto it. The load had to be balanced with care: too much weight in the back of the cart, would lift the horse off the ground, and too much in the front, might break its back! All our work horses were mares and occasionally, they were mated with a visiting race horse stallion. This mixed parentage was known to produce the strong and fast 'hunters' that were highly prized by the local gentry for fox hunting.

When the potatoes were ready to be harvested, women from Leeds were hired by the day. The potatoes were ploughed up with a harrow which was followed by the slowly advancing line of stooped-over women who picked up the exposed 'taters' and put them in baskets – a scene reminiscent of a Breughel painting.

During the winter months the cows were kept inside their stable and were fed on hay and turnips. Since the stone barn (built in the year 1415!) was not large enough for all the hay we constructed haystacks, some 15 feet high, that were covered with a thatched straw roof. Sitting atop a load of hay and holding the reins, as I drove the cart from a distant field to the farm – that was fun, and I recall it now with a smile! It was also fun to ride bareback on one of our patient broad-backed mares. Once, however, while I was riding a mare, its foal insisted on having a snack, whereupon the mare casually tossing me off. I also remember the satisfaction I felt after acquiring the knack of ploughing a perfectly straight furrow for the whole length of the field, followed by the adjoining farrows. Mastering a skill is most satisfying, whatever it may be.

The work in the fields was strenuous but I soon became used to that and it no longer troubled me. It was also very repetitive and boring, leaving me free to daydream, usually about playing a more active role in the war which had by now broken out, but was still in its 'phony' stage (1939/40). The Low Farm practiced 'organic farming' long before that term was fashionable and no chemical fertilizers, pesticides or fungicides ever crossed its lips. The other side of the coin was that we spent long summer days in the grain fields pulling up the hated 'dodge weeds' by hand, and hoeing endless rows of turnips to keep them free of weeds. In winter we hauled the manure that had accumulated in the barn yard to the fields, and spread it with pitchforks. The most disagreeable foul-weather chore was harvesting turnips ('swedes'): they had to be pulled up by their frost-encrusted green tops with the left hand, before they were 'decapitated' by a swift stroke of the sickle held in the right. Gloves were of no use and your fingers were quickly frozen stiff while your back ached from being constantly bent over. The turnips were loaded onto a cart with a pitchfork and were stored for the winter in long, waist-high piles, which were covered first with straw, then with manure, and finally with a layer of soil to keep the turnips from being frozen. In wintertime, we removed this covering and carted the turnips to the farm yard. There we chopped them up in a hand-cranked chopper and fed them to the cows – but they were also a staple at the Morland's dinner table!

My most disagreeable recollection is of having to get out of bed on dark, cold winter mornings to milk the cows – manually, of course. My only diversion was a mouse that opened its mouth for milk that I spurted its way from the cow's teat each morning. After Ken and I finished milking and had mucked out of the stables, we would head for the milk shed where we would each drink a cup of the heavy cream that we skimmed of the top of the previous evening's milk – a pre-breakfast pick-me-up that cardiologists are likely to frown on. After the evening milking we had high tea, listened to the BBC news on the radio and soon went to bed. Sometimes I would stay up to write in my diary by the dim light of a small kerosene lamp that I had bought in Ripon.

The work varied, of course, with the season. For herding the sheep we had the expert assistance of a wonderful sheep dog named Jock, the first, but not the last dog I fell in love with. The sheep had to be dipped periodically to keep their feet from becoming infested with ugly white maggots that could kill a sheep if left unattended. The sheep were confined in pastures surrounded by ancient hedges, and repairing and trimming the hedges with long-handled sharp-edged 'hedgers' was a common chore during the winter months.

Threshing days were exciting and exhausting. In the evening before the appointed day, a self-propelled steam engine that resembled an old-time steam locomotive lumbered into the farmyard, towing a coal tender and the enormous threshing machine. The thresher was powered by means a long looping leather belt driven by the flywheel of the steam engine, and it was parked next to the stack of wheat sheaves. Once the steam was up the thresher required a dozen men to keep it running and the additional requisite manpower was provided by the neighboring farms. Ken, Tom and I got up well before dawn so that all the milking and foddering chores were done before our guest workers arrived. The boiler was then stoked up, the thatching was removed from the stack and two men on top of the stack began pitching sheaves into the machine. Others had the job of hauling away the grain, the straw, and the chaff that spewed out of different orifices of the thresher at an alarming rate. Everyone worked very hard to keep the machine running at top speed in order to avoid a much dreaded, time-wasting 'hold-up.' I had the dirty and itchy job of shoveling the chaff disgorged by the machine into canvas sacks and carrying them into the barn. In mid-morning there was a brief break for a 'drinking', and at noon, to everyone's relief, the monstrous machine came to rest, as did its human attendants. After washing off the soot and grime we sat down at tables that were set up in the orchard, while Ada and the other village women outdid one another in providing a sumptuous lunch to the visiting workmen.

My weekly pay was half-a-crown (or 2/6 shilling) and after a few months it was raised to a crown (5 shillings) which, at that time, was in the shape of a substantial silver coin, worth about one US dollar. After saving enough money, I spent 17 shillings on a bike which needed some repair work but then gave me much greater freedom of motion. On Sundays, after finishing my chores, I could now ride to the ancient cathedral town of Ripon, a few miles away, and go to the cinema there. On Rosh Hashanah I went even further afield for I was invited to attend a synagogue in Harrogate and to have a meal with a local Jewish family. The Harrogate congregation must have discovered my whereabouts through a refugee committee in London that was apparently keeping track of me.

Bishop Monkton had a community center for men, known as the Mechanics Institution (mechanics was the 19th century term for working men), and on Saturday evenings, Ken and I would go there to play snooker. Its female counterpart, the Women's Institute, occasionally organized a 'Whist Drive and Dance', a high point of Bishop Monkton's social calendar. Whist is a card game that resembles bridge in that it is played by two pairs of partners facing each other across the table, but there is no bidding as in bridge. In a whist drive, the winning partners moved to the next table after each hand, ensuring a thorough mingling of all participants. Afterwards there was dancing to the popular songs of the day played on the piano, songs that reflected the still young war: *'We're Going To Hang Out Our Washing on the Siegfried Line', 'It's a Long Way to Tipperary', 'Don't Sit Under the Apple Tree with Anyone Else but Me', and 'When the Lights Go On Again, All Over the World'.* There would be a long wait for that.

By 1940 many of the young men of the village were being drafted into the army and young women from the Land Army made their appearance to take their place. One of them, a dark-haired damsel, Peggy by name, worked on the neighboring farm and awakened my first tentative interest in girls.

There were other social demands on me. One day, I returned from the fields to find the farmhouse abuzz with excitement: Captain Fox's chauffeur had called to invite me to dine with the Captain, and the Morlands were not a little proud of their squire's benevolent gesture: he had evidently spotted me in the village and wished to make my acquaintance. Dressed in my best suit of clothes (knickerbockers!) I was picked up in a large car and driven to Captain Fox's manor house, just outside the village. I was quite unprepared for Captain Fox's friendliness and the lavishness of dinner – we faced each other across the table and ate from gold plates, with a footman standing behind each of us. When I left, I was even more surprised when he kissed me good-bye. That struck me as curious, but then I was in a country with many strange customs! At our third meeting the Captain suggested a game in which he would try to guess my weight by lifting me and feeling my muscles and then suggested that we go upstairs to check the accuracy of his guess on his bathroom scale. Only then did his amorous intentions dawn on me and he proceeded to make them more specific: if I would be more cooperative, he would use his influence at the Foreign Office to secure visas for my parents who were still stuck in Vienna. This put me in a terrible quandary for several days, but since Germany and England were now at war, I had serious doubts that he could actually procure visas for them, and discounted his offer as a ruse. Needless to say, my dinner invitations ceased.

The winter of 1939/40 was unusually cold and miserable in England. I sported chilblains on my feet and gradually reached the conclusion that I did not relish a career in farming. I felt the need for a change in my condition but had no idea how to go about it. Until now I had always done what I was told to do, most recently by the officials of refugee committees, and to act independently did not come easily. Fortunately Lesley, who was at that time working as the receptionist at the Park Royal Hotel in Brighton, wrote me that the hotel had a vacancy for a 'trainee' and I decided to try my luck in the hotel business. As it turned out, the job description was wildly misleading since my primary duty consisted of washing dishes, but the move to the south coast was to have momentous consequences. After agonizing painfully for a long time, I gave notice to the Morlands – who were not at all happy and let me know it.

MY DIARY

In reminiscing about life at the Low Farm, I recalled events that had been stored away for some sixty years, and since my historical research work taught me the importance of primary sources, I dug up the old diary I had begun shortly after arriving in Bishop Monkton. As I read it, I realized that these contemporary, albeit puerile musings and observations may provide a more faithful picture of my state of mind at that time, than my recollections.

I find some of the diary entries embarrassing; it is not easy to identify oneself with a child across a gulf of six decades. I had always been very secretive about the diary (and seem to be so still!) although there was no need to fear prying eyes on the Low Farm, since I wrote in German. This allowed me to get some uncomplimentary comments about the Morlands off my chest. Here then, some selected entries in faithful translation, beginning with the very first.

[22 Oct. 1939]

Dear Diary!

I decided to begin keeping you out of loneliness. That sounds a bit puffed up, but that's the way it is. I hope you will be a good friend to me that consoles me during sad hours. I am fond of you and it will be your task to hang on to all my memories and adventures, so that you will become more valuable to me than to anyone else, for I acquired you at Woolworth's for 3 d. I hope this will do as an introduction and that you will soon get to know me better.

I am at present in a miserable little village in England and work as a "lad" for a humble farmer, Mr. Morland by name. That, in a nutshell is my present position and I will now explain how I got here and why I am writing in German.

I am a Viennese. I was born in Vienna, went to school in Vienna, experienced my childhood in Vienna, was happy and unhappy in Vienna, in short I am a Viennese.

After describing where I lived and where I went to school, I listed the members of my family including, very affectionately, Idi, of whom I have spoken above, interrupting the entry with:

[on a Sunday] Just now the Old Lady [Mrs. Morland] is calling, it's 4 o'clock and I have to go and fetch the cows. I'll continue as soon as I have time.

[25 Oct 1939] If my German occasionally sounds a little fractured, it is because I am unfortunately slowly forgetting my mother tongue.

I forgot to mention that from 1934 to 1938 I was an enthusiastic boy scout, and even though no longer active, I still am. My father, better Pips, is a sweet individual and my mother, better Mutz, is also, in a word, one is sweeter than the other and the day we will meet again will be the happiest of my life.

Pips' family comes from Kostel in Moravia. He spent 7 years in the [Austrian] army and had a neat shop on Hoher Markt 12, where one could buy sponges and chamois until 10 November 1938. The 10th of November was a black day and I know that I will not forget it, and so I don't need to refresh my memories. Pips is also a clever watchmaker.

Mutz comes from Skotschau in Silesia, where until recently my grandmother lived. When Hitler invaded Poland, she had to flee and I don't know where she and the other relatives who lived in Bielitz are. I don't want to write Mutz's biography, the most important thing about her is that she would not change places with 10 Rothschilds once she gets into bed. With Ilse [Lesley] I fought a lot when we were children, but we like each other all the same. She came to Mr. de Costa in London in September 1938 where she was at first very happy, but not any longer.

When Hitler annexed Austria in March 1938, I was still in school and I took all that not very seriously at first. I was still too childish, spoilt, and playful. In many respects I am still childish, in others, I have changed.

After leaving school I lived through a period during which I did almost nothing other than read, go to the cinema (although forbidden), went for walks, in a word, anything other than work. I think I do more work now in a day than I did in a month then. . . .

I then describe how I came to England and how spent my first month in London until:

. . . I got the Committee to send me to a school. It was the Stoatley Rough School in Haslemere where I really had to do hard manual labor for the first time. I was happy to get away from there, but now I would be glad to be back. From there I was sent here and had looked forward to it. But being here for a while I was disappointed and long for the day when I can get away again. It was here that I received my first wages (sh 2/6). Apart from myself, there are two other "German boys" here, Hermann, a nice chap, and Josef, whom I cannot stand . . .

[29 Oct. 1939] To-day is Sunday and one doesn't know what to do. The weather is horrible and my hands are freezing cold at work and back at the house there are these stupid two-faced people – I really miss just one thing, my mother. I wish I were with her again.

To-morrow I will probably get myself a radio, I hope it will give me pleasure.

. . . I received an invitation to a Chanukah party [in Harrogate]. I hope I can go. It is the first Chanukah without the sweet parents. It was Mutz's birthday and I couldn't even write. It's terrible.

I inquired about the cost of visiting London, the bus fare is 26/6. I do have enough money but afterwards I'd have hardly anything left. Besides, I don't know where I could sleep...

[26 Nov. 1939] On Wednesday a fourth German [refugee] arrived here. I spend my evenings at the [Mechanics] Institution or stay at home. I received a very welcome food parcel from Tante Else. I still don't know anything definite about the London trip.

[3 Dec. 1939] I heard from Ilse, unfortunately I cannot stay with her. I am terribly sorry. She doesn't seem to be doing well, I'll send her some money. It's really revolting to think about all that. But I always tell myself that one-day things will be better.

[24 Dec. 1939] . . . Very sadly, I did not go to London, but it cannot be helped "Glücklich ist / wer vergisst / was nicht mehr zu ändern ist" [Happy he who forgets what can't be altered, -- an aria from the Fledermaus]. I was in Harrogate for a Chanukah party on the 10th. I heard from the parents that they may be going to Palestine, I am waiting to hear details. I was at a dance on the 15th, it was nice, a bit of a change. I met a Land Army girl there and didn't get home until 2 am. I also bought myself a bicycle for sh 17/- but I must first repair it.

To-morrow is Christmas and we are off work until Tuesday; that is, I need spend only half of the day milking, foddering and cleaning out the stables. . .

I now have new friends here, Mr. and Mrs. Riley, the postmaster. I give them German lessons.

[31 Dec. 1939] . . . Peggy [the Land Army maid] had left before Christmas. Yesterday I was in Ripon with her. She is finally an intelligent girl whom one can talk with and I am glad to have met her. To-night is New Years Eve and while it will hardly be as nice as former ones, I am very determined as I begin 1940, and where there is a will, there is a way. But I must always have a goal, for if one accepts things as they are and does not strive on, this whole life is without sense of purpose.

I have still heard nothing definite about the dear parents. The niggardly old man and lady did not give me a raise. I sent out 20 Christmas cards, received just 3, from the de Costas, from Evelyn and Mrs. Riley, who also gave me my only Christmas present, a handkerchief.

[7 Jan. 1940] To-day is Ilse's birthday and I sent her a birthday telegram. Unfortunately I am too broke to buy her anything, having spent an awful lot last week. I was again dancing, had to get my bike repaired, I was 2x in Ripon. Unfortunately, P[eggy] left to-day, I am very sorry, we are and remain good friends and it is possible that she will find a job nearby; then we could see each other again.

But the thought of getting away from here occupies me more and more. The old man and lady and the elder son are becoming unbearable and are really getting on my nerves. Yesterday I got a food packet from the de Costas and 2 sweaters besides.

[17 Jan. 1940] To-day I am not at all well, I have an awful grippe. Yesterday I was in bed with a fever, to-day at noon I began to work a little, but it did me no good. I only wish I could get away. Yesterday it snowed and it is terribly cold. It's punishing to work in this weather . . .

[25 Jan 1940] To-day I finally got a letter from the parents, they are in Bratislava and are waiting to continue on to Palestine. To be sure, the letter is from 28 Dec. Now that they have left Vienna and gave up the flat, another thread tying me to Vienna is broken, but I haven't given up hope to go back there one day. I am back in good health but have such an awful chilblain that I can hardly walk.

[28 Jan. 1940] . . . The weather has not improved, it's still snowing and it is England's worst winter since 1894.

[11 Feb. 1940]   I have very important news for you, dear diary, for yester-
day I gave notice!! Lesley has a job as receptionist and bookkeeper in a hotel in
Brighton and I have a job in the kitchen of the same hotel.   I hope that the
Committee doesn't give me any trouble and that I can accept it.   In any case, I
won't stay here, for the old man and lady behaved scandalously when I told them
that I was leaving. But I don't care about all that any more, I tell myself, it won't
be long now, only 4 weeks. I await the Committee's answer with impatience and
pray that it is favorable. . . I finally heard from the parents in Bratislava, they
have to wait until the Danube thaws and they are interned.
[29 March 1940]   I have arrived in Brighton and was terribly pleased to see Ilse
again. About my job here I'll write as soon as possible, but I am too tired now.

NOTES

[1]Among the 65,000 Austrian victims of the Holocaust were nine members of my immediate family: my grandmother, five of my father's siblings, two of my mother's, and one cousin. Remarkably, my eleven other cousins managed to survive.

[2]The Diamant family survived the war intact. They had escaped across the border to Yugoslavia where Hans joined the partisans. After the war Hans returned to Vienna and had a medical practice in a district of Vienna where many Croats lived and Styra and I visited him there in the 1980s. As we left he gave us a bottle of Slivovic, taking it from a closet that was filled with similar bottles, all brought to him by patients on their medical visits - which were, in any case paid by the national health insurance.

[3]The looting of Jewish-owned property and the 'aryanization' of Jewish-owned businesses took place initially on individual initiative and later, in a very systematic and bureaucratic process, documented by Tina Walzer and Stephan Temple (*Unser Wien*, Aufbau Verlag, Berlin). I obtained from the Austrian state archive copies of the form Papa had completed, along with all Austrian Jews, which lists all his possessions - to facilitate their subsequent confiscation (*c.f.* Appendix II).

[4]For an account of the Jewish refugee community in Shanghai during the war see: *Shanghai Refuge* by Ernest G. Heppner (University of Nebraska Press, 1994). Although Shanghai required no visas, a visa to a final destination was essential before one could apply for the necessary transit visas through other coun-tries. Thousands of Chinese visas were issued by the exceptional Chinese consul in Vienna, Feng Shan Ho, who acted out of compassion and in defiance of his superiors. He was responsible for saving the lives of thousands of Viennese Jews, including my cousin Oskar and his wife Bertl.

[5]The astonishing story of the illegal transports has been told by the initial organizer William R. Perl (*The*

Four-Front War (1978, ISBN 0-517-53837-7). Perl miraculously survived the war, emigrated to the United States and became a lawyer in Washington. He inscribed my copy very shakily--he suffered from Parkinson's disease-- shortly before he died in 1999.

After the war, members of Israel's Mossad discovered Eichmann living in Buenos Aires. They abducted him to Israel where he was tried, convicted, and executed (*c.f.* Appendix II).

6 The *Kindertransport* story is told in *"And the Policeman Smiled"* by Barry Turner (ISBN 0 7475 0620 5); it has also been told in the words of many *Kinder*, including this one, in *"I Came Alone, The Stories of the Kindertransports"* by B. Leverton and S. Lowensohn, eds. (ISBN 0 86332 566 1).

7 Idi came from Breslau (now, Wroclaw) in Silesia. When Lesley was born, Omama in Skotschau arranged for Idi to come to us in Vienna. Seventeen years later, after Hitler annexed Austria, Idi rediscovered her German roots. How ironic: When Styra and I visited Breslau/Wroclaw in 1990, it had become so thoroughly Polish that we could not find any German speakers, nor a single German inscription on a building to remind one that this had been an ancient German university town for centuries.

8 Margaret Morland, Ken's widow, recalls that drinkings had to be served punctually at 10 and 3 and that they included sandwiches, pies and tea. If they were delayed, she said, there were "mutterings" among the men. I was reminded of this when many years later, I spent time working in the library of the Wellcome Institute in London, where the lady with the teacart appeared in the corridor outside the reading room, punctually at 10 and 3 every day. One day, she was 15 minutes late and I noticed restive "mutterings' among the scholars in the reading room.

Zur Beachtung!

1. **Wer hat das Vermögensverzeichnis einzureichen?**
Jeder Anmeldepflichtige, also auch jeder Ehegatte und jedes Kind für sich. Für jedes minderjährige Kind ist das Vermögensverzeichnis vom Inhaber der elterlichen Gewalt oder von dem Vormund einzureichen.
2. **Bis wann ist das Vermögensverzeichnis einzureichen?**
Bis zum 30. Juni 1938. Wer anmelde= und bewertungspflichtig ist, aber die Anmelde= und Bewertungspflicht nicht oder nicht rechtzeitig oder nicht vollständig erfüllt, setzt sich schwerer Strafe (Geldstrafe, Gefängnis, Zuchthaus, Einziehung des Vermögens) aus.

3. **Wie ist das Vermögensverzeichnis auszufüllen?**
Es müssen sämtliche Fragen beantwortet werden. Nicht= zutreffendes ist zu durchstreichen. Reicht der in dem Vermögensverzeichnis für die Ausfüllung vorgesehene Raum nicht aus, so sind die geforderten Angaben auf einer Anlage zu machen.
4. **Wenn Zweifel bestehen,** ob diese oder jene Werte in dem Vermögensverzeichnis aufgeführt werden müssen, sind die Werte aufzuführen.

38677

Verzeichnis über das Vermögen von Juden
nach dem Stand vom 27. April 1938

des **E i s i n g e r   Rudolf**   , **Kaufmann** (Beruf oder Gewerbe)
der   (Zu= und Dorname)

in **W i e n**   , III. **Reisner** ============Straße, Platz Nr. **29**
(Wohnsitz oder gewöhnlicher Aufenthalt)

Angaben zur Person

Ich bin geboren am .... **9. Mai 1883**
Ich bin Jude (§ 5 der Ersten Verordnung zum Reichsbürgergesetz vom 14. November 1935, Reichsgesetzbl. I S. 1333) und — deutscher[1] — Staatsangehörigkeit[1] — staatenlos[1] —
Da ich — Jude deutscher Staatsangehörigkeit[1] — staatenloser Jude[1] — bin, habe ich in dem nach= stehenden Vermögensverzeichnis mein gesamtes inländisches und ausländisches Vermögen angegeben und bewertet[1].
Da ich Jude fremder Staatsangehörigkeit bin, habe ich in dem nachstehenden Vermögensverzeichnis mein inländisches Vermögen angegeben und bewertet[1].

Ich bin verheiratet mit .... **Grete Eisinger** .... geb. **Lindner**
(Mädchenname der Ehefrau)

Mein Ehegatte ist der Rasse nach — jüdisch[1] — nichtjüdisch[1] — und gehört der **jüdischen** Religionsgemeinschaft an.

Angaben über das Vermögen

I. Land= und forstwirtschaftliches Vermögen (vgl. Anleitung Ziff. 9):
Wenn Sie am 27. April 1938 land= und forstwirtschaftliches Vermögen besaßen (gepachtete Ländereien u. dgl. sind nur aufzuführen, wenn das der Bewirtschaftung dienende Inventar Ihnen gehörte):

Lage des eigenen oder gepachteten Betriebs und seine Größe in Hektar? (Gemeinde — Gutsbezirk — und Hofnummer, auch grundbuch= und katastermäßige Bezeichnung)	Art des eigenen oder gepachteten Betriebs? (z. B. landwirtschaftlicher, forstwirtschaftlicher, gärtnerischer Betrieb, Weinbaubetrieb, Fischereibetrieb)	Handelte es sich um einen eigenen Betrieb oder um eine Pachtung	Wert des Betriebs RM	Bei eigenen Betrieben: Wenn der Betrieb noch Anderen gehörte: Wie hoch ist Ihr Anteil? (z. B. ¼)
1	2	3	4	5

II. Grundvermögen (Grund und Boden, Gebäude) (vgl. Anleitung Ziff. 10):
Wenn Sie am 27. April 1938 Grundvermögen besaßen (Grundstücke, die nicht zu dem vorstehend unter I und nach= stehend unter III bezeichneten Vermögen gehörten):

Lage des Grundstücks? (Gemeinde, Straße und Hausnummer, bei Bauland auch grundbuch= und katastermäßige Bezeichnung)	Art des Grundstücks? (z. B. Einfamilienhaus, Mietwohngrundstück, Bauland)	Wert des Grundstücks RM	Wenn das Grundstück noch Anderen gehörte: Wie hoch war Ihr Anteil? (z. B. ¼)
1	2	3	4

[1] Nichtzutreffendes ist zu durchstreichen.
Vermögensverzeichnis (DV v. 26. 4. 38).

The first page of a questionaire in which all Austrian Jews were required to list all their possessions, filled out by Papa, barely six weeks after the Anschluss.

Finanzamt Landstraße Wien
(Dienststelle)

_____ 1915-50 III
(Aktenzeichen)

15. April 1939
(Ort und Datum)

3. Schlachthausg 54
(Straße)

Steuerliche Unbedenklichkeitsbescheinigung
(Gültigkeitsdauer: zwei Monate ab Ausstellung)

Gegen die Ausreise des(r) _Eisinger Josef Israel Schüler_

3. Kundenweg 6 _____ (Beruf, Stand, Vor- und Zuname) _____ geboren am 13. 1939 in Wien

(Wohnung)

und seiner Ehefrau _____, geboren am _____

in _____, und seiner Kinder _____, geboren am _____

_____, geboren am _____, geboren am _____

habe ich keine Bedenken.

(Unterschrift)

Lager-Nr. 954. Kleinkonzept 1938. — A 4 (Unbedenklichkeitsbescheinigung). — Staatsdruckerei Wien. (St.) 10.930 38

This is the infamous Steuerliche Unbedenklichkeitsbescheinigung required of all emigrants. It is made out to Josef Israel Eisinger, pupil. After the Anschluss all Jewish males had to add Israel to their name, and all females, Sarah.

Two recent arrivals in Britain, 1939.

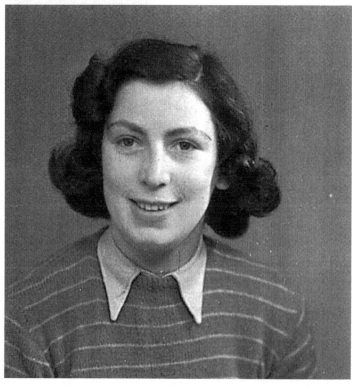

Whist drive and dance at the Women's Institute in Bishop Monkton, Boxing Day, 1939.
I am behind the 3rd fellow from the left in the front row. Photo from the local newspaper.

An old photo showing the kind of farm cart we used for hauling everything from turnips
to hay, although ours were larger and our horses were not as scrawny as this one. The
girl partly hides the man pitching a sheaf to the one on top whose job is to keep the load
balanced. The dog looks a lot like old Jock.

3

INTERNED. IN CANADA.

"COLLAR THE LOT"

Although Britain and France had been at war with Germany since the invasion of Poland in August 1939, the Western front, anchored by France's 'impenetrable' Maginot Line, had remained eerily quiet, giving wing to the notion of a 'phony war'. All this changed dramatically when German armies occupied Denmark and Norway in April 1940, and then invaded the Netherlands and Belgium in the following month, outflanking the French army and the British Expeditionary Force (BEF). The BEF became isolated and surrounded on the beaches of Dunkirk, and it was only thanks to a hastily assembled flotilla of small ships and boats of every description, that the greater part of the BEF was able to escape across the Channel to safety – in my footsteps, as it were.

In the aftermath of fall of France, justifiable fears of the coming German invasion swept through Britain, and rumors circulated of the existence of a 'Fifth Column' of Nazi saboteurs, said to be disguised as refugees and tourists. In this atmosphere the British government decided to take no chances, and ordered the internment of all 'enemy aliens' aged 16 to 60, who lived within 50 miles of the coast. This applied to anyone holding a German passport and no attempt was made to distinguish between Jewish or political refugees and other German nationals. Churchill authorized the operation with the inimitable phrase: "Collar the lot!"[1]

I had just turned sixteen and was working in the kitchen of the Park Royal Hotel in Brighton. Hired as a trainee for the hotel trade, the position seemed to hold greater promise than that of farm hand, and I made the career change with the support of Lesley, as well as Dr. Stefan Kimmelmann, our former neighbor in Vienna, who now lived in Brighton and counseled me in *loco parentis*.

My chief duty was washing the dishes, pots and pans of a substantial residential hotel that served four meals a day to some hundred guests. Dishwashing machines had yet to be invented, and I had to deal with the meter-high stacks of dirty plates and cups that accumulated after each meal, washing, rinsing and drying them by hand. Apart from that, I was responsible for preparing tea in silver-plate teapots in my pantry. The waiters used a buzzer code to let me know the kind of tea (Indian or Chinese) and the size of teapot they were ordering. My other duties included preparing Melba toast[2] and cleaning vegetables when called upon by the chef Marcel, a temperamental Frenchman. Marcel engaged in frequent noisy spats with 'Madam', the owner of the hotel, which usually ended with him threatening to quit on the spot and making his point by packing up his knives; but he never did quit.

My wages were now a formidable 10 shillings (about $2.50) a week, and I slept on a cot in the window-less boiler room in the basement of the hotel. In theory, I was off-duty on one afternoon a week, with the understanding that Pat, the hotel porter, a large brawny Irishman, would cover for me. On my first free afternoon I went to visit the Kimmelmanns and the De Costas who lived in nearby Hove, but when I returned to the hotel, the dirty tea and dinner dishes were stacked all over the pantry floor. I remonstrated with Pat whose response was a curt "fuck off!" and since Madam considered Pat to be harder to replace than me, she declined to get involved in the controversy, leaving me little choice but to forget about afternoons-off. Except for a blissful few hours between the lunch and tea dishes, I spent each day in the pantry from 6 am to 9 pm.[3]

The Kimmelmann family had lived in the same house in Vienna and their son Hans and I had been friends for a long time. He was attending a (private) public school in England when the Anschluss took place, and his parents had managed to follow him to England soon afterwards. They had put me up in their London flat during my first few days in England and Hans's father, a scholarly lawyer in Vienna, had tried very earnestly to assess what professions offered the best chance for economic survival in the bewildering new world we faced. Having concluded that agriculture was the wave of the future, he placed Hans in an agricultural college and he kindly offered to do as much for me, on condition that I first spend one year working on a farm. While the prospect of attending a college had great appeal for me, a return to farming so soon after I had put it behind me, did not. Hans, however, did study agriculture, changed his name to John Keeble and became a specialist on breeding livestock artificially.

Hans and I met in Brighton for the first time since leaving Vienna and we spent many hours talking. This was at the time of the 'phony war' and I gather from my diary that we made plans to return to Vienna together – as soon as the war was over. Evidently, neither of us suspected what a devastating path laid ahead.

In view of my questionable prospects at the Park Royal Hotel, it won't be difficult to understand why I was not greatly distressed when one day, two policemen looked me up in my pantry and asked me politely to accompany them to the police station. I assumed that I was being summoned to fill out another registration form related to my status as enemy alien, I dried my hands, and left the sink full of dishes to join them, when one of the policemen suggested that I might want to bring a toothbrush along. The date was May 16, 1940, shortly after the Dunkirk evacuation, and it finally dawned on me that my life was about to take another sharp turn. Many thoughts must have gone through my mind on our way to the police station, but one that I recall with great satisfaction was the realization that the detested Pat would be doing the dinner dishes that evening! God's in his heaven and all's right on Earth.

At the police station I found myself among a dozen or two of other "enemy aliens" who had been rounded up that day, almost all of them Jewish refugees. Later in the evening, a police van took us to the Brighton racecourse, the first of several improvised internment camps that I was to inhabit in the next twenty months. We were brought into a large hall with a cement floor and were issued cotton pallets which we filled with straw that had been piled high in a corner of the hall. When stuffed with just the right amount of straw, the pallets made acceptable bedsteads.

Lesley had been fired by Madam shortly before my arrest and was now working as an assistant matron at a private boarding school for girls in Brighton.

She obtained permission to leave a package of clothes and food for me at the racetrack gate, but we were not see each other again until the war was over.

I was surprised to run into Dr. Kimmelmann in the Brighton racetrack camp. While I looked on internment as an interesting new experience, he was deeply anguished by it. My experiences so far gave me confidence that I could handle whatever I was likely to encounter while in custody. I never lost sight of the difference between a British internment camp and a Nazi concentration camp – and felt fortunate to find myself in the former.[4] But for Dr. Kimmelmann, internment meant an unacceptable loss of dignity and separation from his lovely wife, Anni. He had always taken a fatherly interest in me in Vienna, as the following incident shows: it took place when I was ten and had just become a student at the prestigious *Akademisches Gymnasium*. Dr. Kimmelmann was on his way home when he saw me riding my scooter in the opposite direction, on an errand to our grocer down the street. He stopped me and reminded me that it was unseemly for a *Gymnasiast* to use a scooter for transportation – well-meant advice in class-conscious Vienna. He tried to improve my mind, as well as my deportment in public, by introducing me (with limited success) to the writings of Nietzsche and Schopenhauer. When we met again at the racetrack in Brighton, I was able to repay his kindness by filling his straw pallet for him.

"STONE WALLS DO NOT A PRISON MAKE…"

There are good reasons why internment caused me little anguish in the beginning, in spite of being deprived of the limited liberty and privacy I had enjoyed at the hotel. I was suddenly freed from the drudgery of my previous jobs, and most important, I found myself in the company of boys of my own age and background for the first time since leaving Vienna. And beyond that, although I did not know it, internment was to open new vistas for me, vistas that would shape the rest of my life.

From the Brighton racetrack we were shipped by train to another camp, an unfinished housing development in Huyton, a suburb of Liverpool. Since there were not enough habitable houses to hold all inmates, the youngest ones, myself included, had to sleep on the ground in pup tents. More distressing was the diminutive food allowance. Our daily ration was a single, inch-thick slice of white bread, occasionally supplemented by a spoonful of jam or a salt herring fished out of wooden barrel. For the first time in my life I experienced hunger for days on end. While attempting to trisect my daily bread ration so I would have a slice of bread for three 'meals' a day, I sliced off a piece of my left thumb and I still retain the scar as a reminder. It was in Huyton that I made contact with Walter Kohn who, although he was a year older, had been a fellow student at the *Akademisches Gymnasium*. We quickly formed a friendship that lasted for more than seven decades.

What follows is a (translated) entry of the diary I had begun in Bishop Monkton.

[End of May 1940] Since my last entry an enormous number of things have changed. First of all, two weeks ago I was arrested and taken to a camp together with 160 other Germans and Austrians. That was at the Brighton racecourse, where everything went comparatively well. I worked in the kitchen together with Dieter and Heinz whom I met there and we had plenty of good food. After 5 days we were, however, sent here and since then I have been hungry, along with many others. We are in Huyton, near Liverpool, and we slept at first on actual beds in real houses. But today we had to give up our beds and all of us under 25 have to move into tents. The food is terrible and there is too little, but otherwise I am fine.

In the meantime the war is going badly for the English. Norway was partly abandoned, Holland and Belgium became Hitler's latest victims, and German troops have occupied Northern France.

Life here is really getting on my nerves, although I have met a lot of nice people. But not being free is awful and you become aware of the value of freedom only after losing it.

After a month in the Huyton camp, we were on the move again. We were marched from Huyton to the Liverpool docks and boarded a ship that took us across the Irish Sea to the seaside resort of Douglas on the Isle of Man.

Our camp there consisted of a few city blocks of mostly small hotels on the seaside that had been requisitioned by the government. The hotel rooms had been emptied of all furniture, including beds, and a double row of barbed wire fences had been erected down the center of the streets that formed the camp's perimeter. We were therefore able to observe the citizens of Douglas pursuing their normal daily life on the other side of the street and the wire, while they, in turn, scrutinized us with interest.

To our amazement, the room I shared with Walter and another friend, Rudi Cohen, contained a working pedal harmonium that had been left behind when the room was stripped of its furnishings, probably, because it was too heavy. The news of the harmonium's existence, the only keyboard instrument in the camp, spread quickly and we were soon beleaguered by a horde of frustrated keyboard players. After a few days we had to enforce a strict ban on music-making after 9 pm.

Although we remained in Douglas for only one month, it was there that a camp "culture" took shape. The inmates sorted themselves out and formed loose groupings that were based on age or on religious, political, and social leanings. We were free to swap living quarters, as long as both parties agreed, so that like-minded cohorts came to be housed together in Douglas and they retained their identity later, in the Canadian camps. There were readily identifiable cohorts of students, of orthodox Jews, of Catholic priests and seminarians, and of veterans of the Spanish Civil War. One cohort consisted of German commercial seamen with Communist leanings who had mutinied and turned their ships over to the British; and another group, called "the Hollanders", had been together since escaping from Rotterdam in a rowboat, barely ahead of the Nazis. There were more than a few academics and artists among us and it did not take long before numerous lectures and concerts were announced on the camp's bulletin board. This wondrously wide spectrum of humanity also included circus performers and acrobats, e.g. the Blumenfeld twins and the Neumann brothers, who practiced their gymnastic routines every day with impressive dedication.

Life on the Isle of Man was tolerable as far as our physical needs were concerned. Once a day we lined up to receive our skimpy food rations, mostly white bread, powdered milk, sugar, and rice, from which we prepared – what else? – rice pudding in the kitchen of our little hotel. The island must have had a bumper crop of rhubarb, for I recall rhubarb being issued with uncommon largesse. Occasionally groups of internees were taken on walks through the island's lovely countryside, naturally, escorted by armed guards, and on one occasion, we were allowed to swim at the nearby beach, albeit with a Bren (machine) gun mounted prominently above the beach to discourage anyone from swimming too far from shore.

What made Douglas less than a holiday camp was the shadow cast by the dismal war news that leaked into the camp (we had neither radios, nor newspapers). We heard that France had surrendered and that the French refugee camps had been turned over to the Nazis. With the threat of an imminent Nazi invasion hanging over Britain, the pessimists among us feared that the same scenario might well be re-enacted in Britain.

It is therefore not surprising, that rumors of internees being shipped to Canada evoked keen interest, particularly among the young and unattached internees. I call it a rumor, because the destination of these transports was never officially announced and one of the transports actually sailed to Australia.[5] While the selection of inmates to be transported seemed haphazard, the youngest ones were generally selected first. We dredged our memories and pooled our scant information about Canada, our presumed destination, but all we knew for certain, was that Canada contained vast forests, that trappers traveled by canoe on its rivers and lakes, and that its hockey team was the best in the world.

It was a thrill to begin our journey to this unknown place once I and my friends had been selected, and we were in high spirits as we boarded the crowded little steamer that took us from Douglas to Greenock, the port of Glasgow. Our mood became considerably more subdued once we were at sea and our ship was tossed about for hours in the notoriously choppy Irish Sea before it reached the calm waters of Greenock harbor, and was tied up next to a large passenger ship that towered above us. The former Polish passenger liner *M. V. Sobieski* dwarfed our ship, and since it seemed infinitely more seaworthy, we could hardly wait to get onto the steep gangway along her hull and up to her deck. It bemused me that the ship was named for the Polish king who, in 1683, raised the siege of Vienna by the Turks – his name was well-known to every Viennese schoolboy. But after standing in line for several hours (something we had come to accept that as normal procedure) with our goal so near, the news spread that the ship was already overcrowded and could hold no more. But eventually we did get aboard, when we were allowed to change places with a group of married men who were already on board but wanted to remain in England. After a wild scramble eight of us took possession of a small cabin furnished with two narrow double-decker bunks. We were therefore obliged to sleep in shifts during the entire voyage, but during that first night aboard, nobody thought of sleep. Finally, at 4 am on July 5, 1940 the *Sobieski* raised anchor and we sailed off to the New World.

Aboard were about 1,000 civilian internees, as well as 500 German prisoners of war, who were housed in the stern portion of the ship, separated from us by a barbed wire barricade on deck and by locked doors, below deck. The first two days at sea were extremely stormy but once we had recovered from seasickness, we enjoyed the sumptuous fare provided by the *Sobieski's* Polish crew, including such luxuries as real hard-boiled eggs! Our ship was part of a large convoy of merchantmen that was protected from marauding U-boats by several destroyer escorts. Halfway across the Atlantic, one of the *Sobieski's* propeller shafts failed and she fell behind the convoy. One of the destroyers circled us for one day, but then it departed to rejoin the convoy while the *Sobieski* was left to her own devices as she limped westward at half speed. We were very much aware of our perilous situation and lined the railings to scan the sea for a tell-tale U-boat periscope, but none appeared. Could it be that the German submarines let this sitting duck go because they had knowledge of her mixed human cargo?

OH, CANADA

When I came on deck early one morning I had my first glimpse of the American continent. During the night the stricken *Sobieski* had dropped anchor and was now basking in the safe, sun-drenched harbor of St. John, Newfoundland. After a few days, when the necessary repairs had been made, we continued our journey to the west, sailing up the mighty St. Lawrence, past the lush banks and peaceful villages of Gaspé. The enormous size of the river dwarfed anything that European rivers had prepared us for.

Three days later the *Sobieski* docked at Wolfe's Cove, named after the British General who landed there and captured Quebec City in 1759. It is now called Anse-au-Foulon, a mile upriver from Quebec City, and there we finally set foot on the American continent. Once ashore, we were subjected to yet another thorough search of our meager possessions, this time by our Canadian guards who relieved us of any remaining valuables. A train awaited us on a siding near the dock, and after a journey of a few hours, we arrived at the town of Trois Rivieres. From the railway station we were marched through streets lined with curious and sometimes hostile crowds of French-Canadians who had expected fierce Nazi paratroopers, as additional inmates of the POW camp housed in the town's exhibition grounds. They must have been taken aback by our motley crew of civilians, including a contingent of bearded and somberly dressed orthodox Jews; were they cleverly disguised Fifth Columnists? It soon became clear that Britain had merely requested the Canadian government to keep their German prisoners for safekeeping, 'for the duration,' without differentiating between POWs and civilian internees. It was to take a long time to convince the Canadian authorities that almost all of their civilian charges were, in fact, Jewish or political refugees and were passionately opposed to the Nazis.

The camp was already inhabited by genuine German POWs and as we marched into the camp, they welcomed us by serving a meal of hard-boiled eggs and raw bacon. The camp was, as usual, unprepared for our arrival. We were taken to an empty exhibition hall where we slept on straw pallets on the cement floor and where immediately a long line formed in front of the only working toilet. At one end of the hall, tables and benches were set up to serve as the mess, and Walter and I were assigned to dish out food prepared by the camp kitchen. Here and later, in the other Canadian camps, we were issued regular Canadian army rations, as required by the Geneva Convention, rations that seemed unimaginably bountiful after the skimpy wartime fare in England.

We encountered other unheard of amenities, such as showers and a recreation ground where soccer games and other sporting events were quickly organized. But soon fights broke out between Nazis and anti-Nazis and the guards were obliged to erect a barbed wire barrier to separate the two warring factions.

Naturally, we had no contacts with Canadian civilians, but were fascinated by anything that we were able to glean of our new environment. The cavernous exhibition hall in which we lived had very high windows that could only be reached by stacking dining tables on top of each other, and we were able to look out from that vantage point. What we saw was home plate and much of the playing field of the local baseball stadium next to the camp, and since we did not know any of the rules, we had to fathom them by observing the strange actions performed by pitchers, batters and fielders. How could I have foreseen that many years later, I, along with my family, would be avid Yankee fans!

A month later we were on the move again. We were marched to a train waiting on a siding, and boarded its ancient carriages with hard wooden benches and sealed-shut windows. Some twenty-four hours later, we found ourselves, dog-tired, on a siding in New Brunswick's back country, some six hundred miles to the east.[6] It was a murderously hot August day, and the two-hour walk from the railhead along a dusty dirt road through the bush was an ordeal for the older internees among us and we youngsters carried their bags along with our own. When we finally reached our new home, Camp B, it turned out to be a clearing in the dense forest, bordered by a double fence of barbed wire. At the center of the camp was a dusty rectangular parade ground with four unfinished wooden H-huts on one long side, and the hospital hut and recreation hut on the opposite side. An elaborate double gate and guard house was on the short side of the compound and at the opposite end was the mess hall and kitchen. The basic housing unit in Camp B was the H-hut, clad in tar paper with an H as its a footprint. (It was to be my residence again, four years hence, in Canadian Army camps.) Double-decker bunk beds were arrayed along the inside walls of the four arms of the H, while the wash-room, showers and toilets were located in its crossbar. Each of the four living sections accommodated about 50 men and each was heated by a barrel-stove which we fed with birch logs from the surrounding woods. Lying on my upper bunk in the darkness of a bitter-cold winter night, I liked to watch the eerie red glow emitted by the stove and the stove pipe.

When we arrived in Camp B, there was no electricity and only a single working water tap for the entire camp. Fortunately, a powerful thunderstorm brought welcome relief from the heat. In the words of my diary:

(Camp B, 16 August 1940) . . . The train journey was not very pleasant since we were in an ancient carriage. The camp is far from ready and worst of all, there is almost no water. On the day we arrived it rained and we washed in the puddles. In a word, conditions were terrible. You couldn't come near the latrine; the smell would knock you down. Now things are much better. We can even work outside the camp. This morning, for instance, I did carpentry, which was a lot of fun. The workmen and the guards are very nice.

Camp B was, in retrospect, a most enriching experience for me. Even though all internees were required to work every day, our simple life left plenty of leisure time for endless discussions and we formed many friendships, including a few lasting lasting ones. Walter had attended school in England where he had studied physics and he introduced me now to its charms. My serious interest in music also has its roots in Camp B, and this was also where I acquired new manual skills, foremost carpentry and lumberjacking. I found both richly satisfying and they also proved most useful in the years to come, when it came to constructing and maintaining our two family abodes: our venerable 'Minetta Banks' town house built in 1820 in Greenwich Village and 'Cleehill' in the wooded highlands of western New Jersey.

With our arrival at Camp B our frequent moves came to an end and camp life settled into a routine. Our basic needs were provided by our Canadian safe-keepers, the food rations were generous, and occasionally included cases of maple syrup in bottles. That delicacy was, of course, quite unknown to us and we ended up drinking it from the bottle, as you would a soft drink. Indeed, we lived so well that many of us took exception to all this comfort and security while a devastating war was raging, a war in which we had a huge stake. Many among us wanted to join the fight and expressed their frustration in endless debates and in petitions at our frequent hut meetings. It was difficult to select a camp leader who would to speak for such a heterogeneous group – including Yeshiva students, Spanish war veterans, merchant seamen and even a few German monarchists and suspected Nazis. The only objective the majority of inmates shared, was convincing the camp commandant that we were neither Nazis nor POWs, and that we were anxious to contribute to

Canada's war effort.

Working outside the camp afforded a glimpse of the world beyond the wire and it gave the illusion of freedom for a few hours. Outside work, mostly in the forest surrounding the camp, was initially voluntary, but was later made compulsory six days a week. I welcomed it as a change from life in the crowded huts and I preferred it to the 'inside' chores, like scrubbing floors and peeling potatoes. When the political ferment led to work stoppages by the inmates, the camp commandant responded by calling out the guard who entered the camp with fixed bayonets to round up the work parties. Among the creative hiding places during such round-ups was the crawl space under the roof of the huts that we scrambled into through a trap door when the guards entered the compound. This ruse worked very well until somebody fell through the ceiling while the soldiers were searching the hut.

For our work we were paid 20¢ a day in paper camp currency with which we could buy such luxuries as chocolate bars and cigarettes in the camp canteen. We were also able to order books, and I still possess the first book of my eventual library: The Pocket Oxford Dictionary that I bought with a week's earnings.

One week after arriving in Camp B, an informal camp school was organized, largely through the efforts of Dr. William Heckscher, a fellow internee and a distinguished art historian, and with the support of several benevolent refugee organizations on the outside.[7] I joined the school along with about twenty others and took courses in English literature, Latin, physics, and mathematics in preparation for the McGill Junior matriculation exam. As a student enrolled in the camp school, I was excused from work on three mornings a week, and at other times I was a member of the so-called 'post-hole gang', an elite work party that originally specialized in the arduous jobs like digging post holes and trenches in the solidly frozen ground, and later was promoted to perform carpentry work. We built a number of wooden huts using stud construction, some inside and some outside the wire perimeter. I have a vivid memory of watching Fritz Rothberger, a member of our 'post-hole gang' as well as a distinguished mathematician and avid mountaineer, clambering nimbly over the roof rafters of a hut under construction.

In winter, guards armed with rifles escorted us into the woods that surrounded the camp and we used double-edged axes to fell trees, as well as to strip them of their branches. We then carried the logs, often through knee-deep snow, to a clearing where the circular saw was set up. The saw was powered by one of those archaic single-cylinder gasoline engines, known as a 'one-lunger', that required a large flywheel to keep the engine (and the saw) running between the sporadic explosions of the engine – the sound of those irregularly spaced explosions is unforgettable. Our guards, all WWI veterans, were very friendly towards us inmates and since many of them had worked as lumberjacks in civilian life, they acted as our instructors. Their missing fingers and toes were silent witness to the inherent peril of men swinging double-edged axes, in deep snow, and in close proximity to each another!

Later on, in Camp A, we worked at knitting camouflage nets for artillery pieces. We learned our net-making skills from the German seamen among us, many of whom had also been commercial fishermen. I found net-making particularly satisfying, maybe because the net, once it was finished and edged with a rope, represented a personal, tangible contribution to the war effort.

Herewith a few more entries from my diary:

(24 August, 1940) The day before yesterday we were issued toilet articles for the first time (towel, razor, shaving brush, toothbrush, etc.)! What's more, uniforms arrived for us, which we refused, because they had a huge red circle on the back of the blue jacket and shirt. The water shortage is continuing and it is hard to get any water for washing . . . I still have not had a sign of life from Ilse. In England there were heavy bombardments. Today is the anniversary of the German-Russian treaty.

(8 Sep., 1940) At last I had mail from Ilse, unfortunately she has still not heard anything from me. London was victim of horrendous air attacks and I hope this terrible war will soon be over. I have again written to my parents, about whom I know virtually nothing. We must now wear our uniform at work (blue with a big red circle on the back). There is still very little water.

(23 Sep., 1940) For the past 2 weeks I have been working in the soldiers' kitchen which I like very much and where Heinz, Klaus and I spend almost all day. We have good food, a radio, books, and a gramophone there. We had our first payday last week and I received $1.00.

(26 Oct., 1940) The Canadian winter began this week. We had the

first snow a week ago, then had some fine weather and when we awoke to-day everything was white. Yesterday we felled trees again and Walter cut his foot with the ax and is now in the [camp] hospital. To-day we were again given new questionnaires.

(19 Nov., 1940) These days I go out to work rarely and study more instead. I think the latter is more important and I consider the former a waste of time. As life becomes more regular, I suffer more often from "being in a bad mood", but when one thinks clearly about it, that is nothing but a state of mind and a folly. Yesterday I finally had a letter from Ilse, but she knows as little of our parents as I do.

(21 Dec., 1940) Lately I worked a lot, mostly doing carpentry. . . . It has become very cold but we received sufficient clothing. I try to study as much as possible but it is almost impossible to find a spot in the whole camp where one can be alone and can concentrate.

(18 Jan., 1941) We are now forced to work every day and if you want to skip a day, you are chased by the soldiers all day long, in a word it takes as much time to avoid work as to perform it. A few days ago it was terribly cold and the wind howled so that your skin hurt when you went outside, something you avoid as much as possible. The temperature was −17 °F.

(29 March, 1941) I am at the moment preparing for the matriculation exam, which I am planning to take in June. 2 weeks ago I finally had news from the parents, who have arrived in Palestine . . . Our library has grown tremendously and has many fine books. We also got an electric gramophone. The 6 subjects I'm taking for the matric are English, German, Math, History, Latin, and Intermediate Math. I also had a very nice birthday; we had a great party with apple cake and whipped cream etc. As presents I got a pocket knife, socks, chocolate etc. Furthermore, I received news of Mummy and Daddy arriving in Palestine on that very day [19.3.1941].

In camp we generally spoke German to each other, which was, after all, our mother tongue, and up to now, I had also kept my diary in German. But beginning with the next entry, I switched to English, crossing a significant linguistic divide without even noticing it!

(11 April, 1941) Just now I am spending what I consider the best time

I have had during my internment. I am studying all day long and as far as I can judge, am happy doing so . . . It may seem ridiculous, yet summing up, I must admit that I am glad I got interned. Internment and the people I met there have shown me the right way . . . I often wonder what my thoughts respecting my future were before.

(26 June, 1941) I am now in Camp A (Farnham, P.Q.) where we arrived four days ago after a long and wearisome journey of 28 hours. There was a lot of excitement before our departure since the authorities tried to enforce their lists of names, and only in the last minute allowed 5 people to be exchanged, among them Walter.

This camp is very fine . . . There is a lot of work being done here, net making, woodworking, knitting nets, farm work, etc.

(16 July, 1941) I am now doing physics with Walter and have decided to attend the new calculus course for the matric that Rothberger has started. I work every day making nets and since one needs to work only 2 hours a day I have plenty of time for my studies while earning some money. Our status is said to be about to change, from Monday on we will be allowed to use ordinary stationery.

The discussions and the confrontations with the military regarding our POW status continued in Camp A, where we were moved sometime during the summer of 1941. Since this camp was within the town of Farnham and not utterly isolated like Camp B, we mounted a large sign proclaiming our anti-Nazi sentiments on the roof of a hut, which was visible from beyond the wire. We also continued to object to having to wear the prison uniforms and we refused to use POW stationery since it was handled by the Swiss Red Cross along with mail from German POWs. We capitulated on the uniforms, since the approaching Canadian winter left us little choice, but won the right to use plain stationery – all issues that loomed as matters of life and death at the time!

No account of camp life would be complete without mentioning the daily 'roll call' ritual at each of the camps. We assembled on the parade ground twice a day, but counting several hundred chatty prisoners milling around in barely discernible formations, understandably, took a long time. There were many miscounts, but no escapes. One of our camp commandants tried to instill a measure of military discipline into us, and ordered that all internees had to take part in physical exercise parades, twice a day. Although the guards could herd us onto the parade ground with fixed bayonets, it was much harder to make this unruly crowd perform meaningful exercises and after a few days the idea was abandoned.

THE BEGINNING OF THE END

Many well-meaning individuals and organizations had become aware of our Kafkaesque situation and worked to have our status changed from POWs to 'Refugees from Nazi Oppression.' One year after we arrived in Canada, their efforts bore fruit and being released in Canada became a realistic possibility. These benevolent groups also provided books for the camp school and when it turned out that the matric exams had to be written within the city limits of Montreal, they obtained the cooperation of the camp commandant who made it possible: he arranged for Dr. Heckscher and his band of students to be driven by truck and under guard to Camp S, an Italian internment camp that happened to be located in Montreal. The camp became our home during exam week.

Camp S was housed in an ancient fortress on St. Helena's Island (Ile Ste. Hélène) in the middle of the St. Lawrence, and the bridge spanning the river is supported by a massive stone pillar whose footing sits on the island. A few hundred Italians who had been interned in England were housed in dormitories whose five foot-thick walls were pierced by narrow window slits. The walls and buildings of the old fortress enclosed an irregularly shaped courtyard paved with stones and on this, the only open space of the camp, the Italian internees played soccer with an interesting twist: the playing field had no boundaries and balls that bounced off a wall remained in play. The camp had a Fascist leadership, but the civilian inmates – many of them ice cream vendors or waiters who had worked in London – were delighted by the diversion our visit afforded. When we arrived they welcomed us with a huge cake decorated with icing that spelled *'Viva il Duce!'* The Italians invited our group to a friendly game of soccer *á la* Camp S and, predictably, they trounced us soundly. My diary relates what else occurred during our stay in Camp S:

(21 Sep., 1941) . . . But the real thing started on Wednesday at 3:30 hours, when we went by bus to an exquisite club in Montreal. After an interesting drive through Montreal we arrived at the above-mentioned Montefiore Club and all our expectations were surpassed when we met – girls there. We had a gorgeous evening, excellent supper on tablecloths and china plates and cups. We were served by waiters, butlers and maids and the whole thing seemed like a dream to us. There were also some ladies from the Committee there and a few lucky ones found sponsors. I met many nice people and danced once or twice. At last we had to leave the club and with kind words from the guests and gestures from the intoxicated guards we went like chickens back into the barbed wire coop. Brr . . . Back at "A" the next day I was rather depressed and I have never been so desirous to be released . . . Montreal is a pretty city and McGill a beautiful university. Maybe I'll be there some time, but it is too beautiful to be true.

Although it had now become possible for students to be released if a Canadian citizen accepted the financial responsibility of supporting him, this was of purely theoretical interest for most of us. Yet, one month after our excursion to Camp S, I recorded this entry in my diary:

(22 Oct. 1941) Yesterday I received the most wonderful letter I could receive, namely from Mrs. Mendel promising me and Rappa [Walter Kohn] that they would sponsor us! I was just at the dentist's and George [Sanger] was mixing amalgam when Odizetti [Walter Odze] brought the letter and I nearly fell off the chair.

Bruno and Hertha Mendel, both members of a notable German Jewish family of doctors (they were first cousins), had recognized the danger posed by Hitler very early and they, their three children (Gerald, Ruth, and Anita), and Hertha's mother Toni, had left their home in Berlin in 1933. They had eventually settled in Toronto, where Bruno was a medical researcher at the University's Banting Institute. When the Mendels heard of the dilemma of the Jewish refugees in the Canadian camps, they sponsored a total of five students, sight unseen, thereby releasing them from internment. Bruno and Hertha's family had a spare room in their home and invited Walter and me to live with their family. They had chosen us because a previously released internee, Charles Kahn, had told them that in camp, Walter and I played recorder duets together. Being music lovers, the Mendels evidently reasoned that anyone who enjoys music cannot be all bad! It was the first, but not the last instance of music affecting the course of my life profoundly.

But I digress . . .

(3 Nov., 1941) During the last few days I have been awfully depressed and have hardly studied anything. I am getting very impatient and I fear that if this matter should not bring about my release I would get desperate.

(10 Nov., 1941) This is the anniversary of the 10th of November (Kristallnacht) and it was decided to take up a collection for German Jews today . . . and not to eat to-day. This is the 5th day of fasting for me this year. George [Sanger] was released on Saturday 8th XI . . . I had news from Mummy but they were not very cheerful and quite downhearted. It made me sick when I read the letter, I am sorry for her, she is still interned [c.f. Appendix II].

Even though we were now officially 'Anti-Nazi Refugees' and a few internees had actually being released, the cauldron of camp politics continued to bubble. The commanding officer (CO) inevitably became exasperated with the various quarreling internee factions, and we countered his harsh measures with work stoppages. When he retaliated by transferring seven 'troublemakers' to another camp, most of us went on a hunger strike in protest. The strike collapsed after three days, when the CO threatened to halt all further releases. When my release seemed imminent, my friends felt that I needed a nickname that would be more acceptable to Canadian ears than Pepi or Bubi, names I was known by in camp. They held a meeting and after consulting the comic strips in a newspaper they chose Terry, after the hero of *Terry and the Pirates*, a nick-name has stuck to me ever since.

While waiting for the release papers, I gradually became detached from camp life, and the weeks passed very slowly. Finally, early one frosty morning in January 1942, an army truck took me through the double gates of Camp A and deposited me at the Farnham railway station. I was handed $15 (the Mendels were later charged for it) and bought a ticket to Toronto and stood by myself – itself a strange feeling – on the platform, savoring freedom after 20 months of confinement. I was wearing an army great coat, dyed civilian dark blue, a disguise that allowed me to mingle inconspicuously with ordinary men and women – as if that were a perfectly natural thing to do! (It is a sensation that has never left me entirely.)

The train pulled into the station and as I climbed up the steps into the railway carriage, I recall being keenly aware of a new chapter of life beginning.

"MINDS INNOCENT AND QUIET TAKE THAT FOR A HERMITAGE"

Recalling my period of internment while writing these lines was quite evocative, so I may be forgiven for the following musings. I always looked on the time I spent behind barbed wire as a 'good thing' in my life. If emigration had not already done so, internment taught me the value of adaptability in changing environments – a lesson well understood by Charles Darwin, not to mention by my ancestors, all of them survived in environments that were rarely stable or benign.

These months of internment not only set my life on a new course, they also let me feel at home with a wide range of humanity. How else did you get to know circus acrobats, seamen, and mathematics professors on an equal footing? True, the loss of freedom and, just as much, of privacy was painful (even the toilet stalls lacked doors) but there were compensations: We were provided with food and shelter, were on the whole treated humanely, and were relieved of the responsibility of earning a living or being responsible for others. We had time to talk, to read, to acquire new skills, and to make friendship – without being distracted by a job, a family, or women. Indeed, at the very time when war raged in the outside world, we found ourselves in a pseudo-monastic community – a veritable Shangri La!

Some of the friendships made in camp turned out to be lasting ones. After we were released, Walter and I shared a garret in the Mendels' house in Toronto and were students at the University of Toronto, a year apart. We joined the army together and after graduating, we both won fellowships in Cambridge, he at Harvard and I, at MIT. Only after Walter moved to California did our lives diverge, but even after that we met often at scientific meetings and at Bell Labs where he often worked during the summer. I have remained in touch with a few other ex-internees (Walter Michel, Martin Ostwald, George Sanger, Eric Koch, Joe Kates, Paul Pfalzner) with whom I share the bond of a critical common experience. Helmut Kallman, another ex-internee, for a while circulated a newsletter with reminiscences of alumni of the Canadian camps beginning in 1999. The comments that appeared in it showed what a significant role internment had played in our lives and they brought back to mind the days we spent together in camp – not without a tinge of nostalgia.

With regard to music, it was while sitting on the wooden benches in the recreation hut in Camp B that I came to cherish classical music. That is where musician inmates gave occasional recitals, and where we listened to the Sunday afternoon symphony concerts from New York issuing from the camp's only radio sitting on the stage of the recreation hut.[9] Later, when I heard Hertha and Bruno Mendel play Mozart sonatas together, it awakened my desire to play with others. I exchanged the recorder I had bought in camp B, for a wood 'open-hole' flute presented to me by the Mendels, while their friend, the violinist Eugene Kash, kindly donated a few lessons with the Toronto Symphony Orchestra's first flutist. I became sufficiently proficient to play (later on a Böhm silver flute) in the university orchestra and later, in the MIT symphony orchestra. At the time we rehearsed Mendelssohn's "Elijah" at MIT, I happened to be in a very susceptible state of mind and I was so moved by a cello solo (*Ich habe genug...*) that I decided to switch instruments, bought a cello and took a few cello lessons. After I came to New York, I studied with Messrs. Rainer and Rosanoff and joined the Greenwich Village Symphony Orchestra. We rehearsed once a week, usually in Judson Church on Washington Square, and feeling a need for more lessons, I engaged the leader of the cello section – my beloved future wife, Styra. Some say those were the most expensive lessons I had, but for the next fifty years my life has revolved almost as much about music, as about science. Our home has been the site of countless rehearsals and chamber music sessions, most famously of the annual New Year's Day musicales. We hosted those musical extravaganzas at Minetta Banks, beginning in the 1960s, and they continue still (2014).[10] On the musicological side, I found myself participating in an agreeable *ménage-a-trois* with Johannes Brahms for the past thirty years.

I never felt resentful towards Britain for her misguided internment policy in those dark, fearsome days following the fall of France. But other ex-internees, such as the Nobel laureate Max Perutz whom I visited him in Cambridge (1981), were still angry even after the passage of many years. Whether the internment experience was a positive or negative one, depended on one's temperament, but casting blame on a nation for lapses of its government always seemed futile to me, and I shy away from it. I could, for instance, never see eye to eye with my friend George Feher, where England is concerned: having lived in Palestine under British rule, he was embittered by Britain's dreadful immigration policy;[11] while I admired Britain, for in the end, she stood up to Hitler, and was the only nation willing to accept some 10,000 Jewish children who escaped from the Nazis in the *Kindertransport*. But then, I had been one of them.

NOTES

[1] The history of the internment of 'enemy aliens' has been researched and told by my friend Eric Koch in his book *Deemed Suspect (1980,* ISBN 0-458-94490-4); see also: *Collar the Lot* by Peter and Leni Gillman (1980 ISBN 0-7043-2244-?); *A Bespattered Page? The Internment of His Majesty's Most Loyal Enemy Aliens* by Ronald Stent (1980 ISBN 0 233 97246 3); *Auf Sie haben wir gewartet* by E. Sarton-Saretzki, (ISBN 3-928100-55-6); and *Both Sides of the Wire* Vol.1 by Ted Jones (1988, ISBN 0-920483-21-6), which tells the story of camp B from both the prisoners' and the guards' point of view.

[2] To prepare Melba toast, you slice a white toast (carefully!) through its center plane and toast the exposed inner faces in a broiler.

[3] On Pat's day off, I had to take over his porter's duties. On my first day on the job, after I carried the bags of an arriving guest to his room, I was offered a tip which I refused, for I had been taught not accept money from strangers. I wonder what the guest made of that!

[4] My cousin Hilda's husband Ernst Zweigenthal had spent a month in the KZ Buchenwald and was released on condition that he would emigrate immediately. While he and Hilde stayed with us in our flat, and just before they left, he took me aside and after swearing me to secrecy, he told me of the unspeakable degradations and tortures that KZ inmates were subjected to. It left a devastating impression on me. He

had been warned that if he ever spoke to anyone of what he had experienced, he would be sent back immediately. This burly six-foot engineer had returned as a terrified and broken man and soon after he and Hilda had emigrated to Bolivia, he committed suicide.

[5] Four 'prison ships' carried a total of 6,675 internees and prisoners-of-war to Canada. One, the Arandora Star, was sunk by a U-boat, with the loss of 1,000 lives. A fifth ship, the Dunera, transported the Arandora Star survivors and others to camps in Australia. She had a narrow escape when a torpedo glanced off her bow. (Koch, op. cit.).

[6] We did not know it then, but this was Ripples Station, some 20 miles from Fredericton, NB. Curiously, this wartime internment camp site has now become a piece of local history and in nearby Minto, NB, there is a museum to commemorate it.

[7] These included the YMCA, the European Student Relief Fund, the Canadian National Committee on Refugees and various other Jewish organizations. In 1995 Styra and I visited Dr. Heckscher, then a retired faculty member of the Institute for Advanced Study in Princeton. He was then over ninety and full of life, flirting outrageously with every female within his reach.

[8] Walter Kohn's nickname came from his uncle who immigrated to Brazil and changed his name from Rappaport to: Rappa da Porto. Walter became a distinguished theoretical physicist and won the Nobel Prize for Chemistry in 1998.

[9] As one of the few links to the outside world, that wooden radio console played an important part in camp life. This was appreciated by the camp commandant, who would at times punish the inmates collectively by ordering the sergeant major to remove one of the set's vacuum tubes. On December 7, 1941, the concert of the New York Philharmonic was interrupted to announce the attack on Pearl Harbor.

[10] For the record, Minetta Banks is the name Alison gave to our home at 197 West Houston Street. When the house was built in the 1820s, it stood on the banks of the (now subterranean) Minetta Brook, which flows into the Hudson. The musicales there were of impressive size and quality, most musicians being professionals (they let me play because it was my ball). One year, Styra managed to entice all of the instrumentalists needed for the six Brandenburg Concertos – from the strings and a Bach trumpet to French horns and bassoons – and we duly played all six Concertos that New Year's day. We usually started in the afternoon with musicians and listeners crowded into our living room and kitchen. The numbers declined as the evening wore on and by 2 a.m. the ensembles had shrunk to trios and sonatas. We naturally provided a delicious buffet (*Liptauer and Fleischsalat* being traditional favorites), along with beer and wine to nourish the players between musical offerings.

[11] After fleeing from his native Bratislava and making his way to Palestine via the Balkans and Turkey, George had worked against the British in the last days of their mandate by intercepting their telephone conversations and devising a secure communication system for the Haganah.

84

The Polish liner Sobieski that transported us internees and a group of German POWs to the New World.

The melody of our camp song: "You'll get used to it, . . . "

Six friends in Camp B. All were eventually released in Canada as students.
Clockwise from top left: Walter Michel, I, Walter Kohn, Josef (Pepi) Weininger,
George Sanger, and Walter Odze.

In 1940, I was in a group of internees who were confined in the port on St. Helen's Island, Montreal, then an Italian internment camp, to write our matric exams there. This sketch of our view of the city, is from my diary.

Hertha Mendel, 1943.

The fateful letter in which the Mendels invited Walter and me to live with their family in Toronto.

Refugees, who left Germany in 1933 and are now Canadians. My husband is a Physiologist and Professor at the University of Toronto. We have three children of about your age and we are all looking forward to seeing you soon.

With best wishes
Yours sincerely.
Bruno and Hertha Mendel.

Toronto, Oct. 10th '41

Dear Mrs. Kohn and dear Mrs. Eisinger,

I hope you won't mind that we are writing to you both together. We have heard from Charles Kohn that you are great friends and we want to tell you that we would like to be your sponsors and are hoping to have you with us very soon.

I suppose you would like to know who we are. We are German

4

STUDENT AND SOLDIER

AT THE MENDELS

I could hardly have hoped for a more congenial environment than that I found myself in, following my release in January 1942. The family to whom I owed my freedom, Bruno, Hertha and Toni Mendel, were themselves Jewish refugees who had been politically astute enough to leave Germany right after Hitler became German Chancellor early in 1933. Bruno had been a medical researcher in Berlin where he was an associate of the renowned biochemist Otto Warburg. When he emigrated, he gave up his life of a researcher, which-would have become untenable soon enough. He left Germany and went to work for a cosmetics firm, first in Paris, then in Amsterdam, but once the family realized that no country in Europe was safe from Hitler, they moved to Toronto where Bruno found a research position at the University's Banting Institute. He was among the first to purify cholinesterase, an enzyme that plays a crucial role in neuronal transmission and hence, in brain function. After the war, the Royal Society honored him for his contributions which have long since been refined and superseded by subsequent research work – that being the eventual fate, alas, of most scientific research.

Since the Mendels escaped from Nazi Germany so early, they were able to take many of their possessions with them. As a result, their Toronto home retained much of the character of the sumptuous villa in Berlin-Wannsee where they had lived along with Hertha's widowed mother, Toni, the villa's owner. Albert Einstein had been a close friend of the Mendel family, and particularly, of Toni, and he was a frequent visitor there. The intellectual atmosphere that suffused the Mendels' Toronto home and its old-world furnishings were somewhat anachronistic in the very provincial, puritanical Toronto of the 1940s – a very different place from the cosmopolitan city it is today. The house was filled with books, music, and paintings, and I particularly recall a haunting watercolor of two hooded figures by Rabindranath Tagore, the Bengali author and musician whom the Mendels knew in Berlin and had introduced to Einstein. Bruno had arranged two famous discussions between the two men who were widely seen as representatives of Eastern and Western philosophies.

For Walter and me, just emerged from two years of living in barracks, our new home was utopia. Leopold Infeld, an eminent theoretical physicist and a collaborator of Einstein, was then a professor of applied mathematics at the University and a frequent visitor at the Mendels' home.[1] Einstein, who was then living in Princeton, was still corresponding with 'Omama' Toni (as we all knew her), an elegant and lively lady with boundless interest in everything from the arts and science to politics and the war. She lived in nearby Oakville and her home, too, was filled with books, art and music from her Berlin home; I often visited her there by bicycle.[2]

Walter and I shared an attic room in the Mendels' home at 98 Bedford Road, and we quickly became part of the family. Their daughters, Ruth and Anita, were a little younger than we and attended a private school (Bishop Strachan School), while their son Gerald had just graduated from Upper Canada College and was about to be commissioned in the Canadian Army. We kidded around a lot with Ruth and Anita and helped them with their schoolwork, mostly math, and we got along well with the whole family. We even grew accustomed to their North-German accent and their taste in cooking, which struck our Austrian palates as being overly bland.

After I arrived in Toronto, I enrolled in the last (fifth) grade of a public high school (Oakwood Collegiate) and the few months I spent there were my initial contact with Canadian culture. The school was a fair distance from the Mendels' house and I rode to school every day on one of the Mendels' (gearless) Dutch bicycles, often through snow and slush. My teachers were astonishingly different from the *Herren Professoren* who had taught me in Vi-

enna, some of whom had instilled in me more fear, than knowledge. I was unprepared by the informality and friendliness with which the teachers treated
students. This was also the first time that I was in a class together with girls,
a confusing experience for one just emerged from a monastic existence. My
inexperience in dealing with the opposite sex and my awareness of being an
'outsider', left me self-conscious and ill-at-ease with girls, even though they
interested me exceedingly. At school dances, I never knew what to say to my
partner, and I was as inept at the art of small talk then, as I am still.

In May I passed the senior matriculation exams, in effect the entrance
exam of the University of Toronto. The war was, of course, very much on
everyone's mind and it continued to go very badly. With German armies deep
inside Russia and Japanese forces victorious all over the Far East, the news left
me feeling guilty for having no part in the war effort.

Some time after I joined the Mendel family, their household expanded
once again. Kate and Dorothy Simon arrived in Canada as 'war guests' and
joined the little refugee community at 98 Bedford Road. Their father Franz
Simon was a low-temperature physicist whom the Mendels knew from their
Berlin days. The Simon family had also made an early exit from Nazi Germany and had settled in Oxford, where Simon held a research position at the
University.[3] What astonished us all at the time was how frequently Simon
visited his daughters in Toronto, for it was unheard of, that a civilian should
fly across the Atlantic, repeatedly, in wartime! It was only after the war that
we learned that Simon had served as the liaison between British and American
physicists working on the Manhattan Project. After the war he was knighted
for his service, and he is just one of many German-Jewish scientists who made
important contributions to the Allies' war effort. One shudders to consider
what might have happened, had Hitler's anti-Semitism had not deprived him
of all that scientific talent!

The Mendels owned an almost new Oldsmobile sedan with a hydraulic
(automatic) transmission, a great novelty at the time, and I learned to drive
it under Gerald's tutelage. The car was used only rarely, for Bruno treasured
his stash of gas ration coupons and was reluctant to see the car leave the
garage. To overcome his frugal instincts, Walter and I jokingly suggested that
tires that were not exercised regularly would deteriorate, and since we were by
then regarded as technical gurus, Bruno took our counsel seriously and let us

use the car more frequently.

After obtaining my first driver's license, I took a summer job as chauffeur and private secretary to the eminent, long retired Canadian historian, George M. Wrong, who was then in his eighties and virtually blind. After he had been widowed, he had married (to the consternation of the Wrong family) 'Burgy,' who had been the governess of his son's children. In Toronto, George and Burgy Wrong lived only a few blocks from the Mendels, and for the summer they moved to their large Georgian summer home in Canton, Ontario, and I accompanied them there. Apart from serving as their driver, I spent my days reading to Mr. Wrong, taking care of his correspondence, and playing chess with him, using special chessmen that he could identify by touch. These duties left me sufficient time to earn a little extra money by working afternoons at clearing mud out of a millpond. I worked alongside a local villager using high-pressure water hoses, and we got along well enough, except for occasional fierce anti-Semitic diatribes he launched into, while admitting that he had never actually encountered a Jew. I kept my peace until my last day on the job when I told him that I was a Jew – and left him quite literally speechless.

This was my first, but not my last happy association with the Wrong family. Mr. Wrong's granddaughter, June Wrong (later, Rogers) was a close friend when were students together at the university. She introduced me to the University History Club, and I took part in formal debates on long forgotten motions regarding the pressing political issues of the time. She is one of the few fellow students with whom I am still in touch (till 2010). Her brother Dennis is now Professor Emeritus of Sociology at NYU, but I remember him best from our headier days as freshmen at the university. At the end of the spring term, Dennis, Sol Littman (both sociologists) and I found summer jobs working on a Mennonite farm near Niagara-on-the-Lake.[4] We ate and slept in the farmhouse and spent the days weeding and harvesting peaches and tomatoes. The Soviet Union had by then become an ally in the war against Hitler and social fervor ran high among us students. Each morning we marched out to the tomato fields and orchards, singing the 'International' *(Arise, ye prisoners of starvation / Arise, ye wretched of the Earth)*.

Such indiscreet behavior would, no doubt, have scandalized Dennis' father, Hume Wrong, an historian like his father and a senior officer in Canada's

Department of External Affairs. After the war he was appointed Ambassador to the United States. When I was a graduate student at M.I.T. and came to Washington for the annual meetings of the American Physical Society, the Wrongs kindly put me up at the Embassy. I particularly enjoyed that laudable English custom of early morning tea, which was brought to my bedroom by the embassy butler.

The Wrong family spent their summer vacations at a simple cottage on an idyllic little lake in the Gatineau and I recall visiting them there. I was on my way back to Toronto from the North country where I had worked with geophysical techniques to assess the commercial potential of mining claims (of which, more later). It was a lovely late summer weekend which still sticks in my mind with remarkable clarity – possibly, because of a beautiful English girl of about thirteen was also staying at the Wrongs' cottage. I only saw the girl on that one occasion and what remains etched in my memory, is the image of her standing, long-legged in her bathing suit and bathing cap, atop a large smooth rock at the edge of the lake. The reason may be that I learned soon afterwards, that after she had returned to school a week after I had seen her, she died suddenly of a brain tumor.

STUDENT DAYS AND SUMMER JOBS

At the end of the summer of 1942, I registered in the Mathematics and Physics (M&P) honors course at the University of Toronto. I made that fateful choice without giving any thought to physics as a profession, but simply because I appreciated the approach to discovering reality that physics offers.[5] The chaotic years just past may have made science particularly appealing, and my friendship with Walter Kohn surely influenced me, as well. The quest to understand reality – not just physical reality – has remained an important preoccupation of mine.

Several other ex-internees were also students at the university and naturally we stayed in touch with each other. I saw a lot of Walter Michel who had been a close friend in camp (he still is) and who lived in a student co-op, just two blocks from the Mendels' house.[6] In an act of reckless abandon, he and Walter bought an old Model A Ford, which was occasionally operational. It had to be started with a hand crank, or by pushing it, in gear, and releasing the clutch, once it got rolling. Fortunately, it was much easier to push than today's automobiles.

Thanks to the excellent preparation I had received in Camp B's camp school, I was able to keep up with all my courses, but a serious snag developed in obtaining credit for the obligatory course in inorganic chemistry. The chairman of the Chemistry Department considered the ex-internees to be security risks and barred them from entering the chemistry building, supposedly on account of the secret war work going on in there. All chemistry lectures and laboratory classes took place in the chemistry building and the chairman's ruling was widely considered to be motivated more by anti-Semitism than security concerns. Many months of fruitless negotiations between him and the liberal faction of the faculty, headed by my much-loved mathematics professor Sam Beatty, led nowhere. Books and lecture notes allowed me to keep up with the course material, but how was I to perform the required laboratory work? At the end of the term, with all classes officially already finished, the chairman of the Chemical Engineering Department kindly gave me permission to do the laboratry work in the Chemical Engineering building. This is where I performed all the experiments and wrote the lab reports for each in a few days – and nights – working alone in a large, deserted laboratory. To make matters worse, I had caught the flu and I recall stumbling deliriously through the campus on my way home, early one morning after an all-nighter in the lab. To my relief, the reports I churned out were found to be satisfactory, and I received credit for the course. But the experience left me with a certain antipathy towards chemistry which I did not overcome until many years later, when my research turned to molecular biology and I was obliged to learn basic biochemistry.

Apart from chemistry, we had courses in calculus, analytical geometry, and classical physics (mechanics, heat, properties of matter, and electromagnetism) in our freshman year. Other required courses were English Literature (from Chaucer to T. S. Eliot), Religious Knowledge, Military Science, and Actuarial Science to prepare us for employment with insurance companies – at that time, almost the only career open to mathematicians, other than teaching[7]. This being wartime, all male students were enrolled in the Canadian Officers Training Corps (COTC), and on two days a week, we wore our battle dress uniform to classes, were drilled, and had to listen to boring lectures about the army's command structure. At the end of the spring term, we spent two weeks living under canvas in a COTC training camp, and took part in marches and field exercises.

Since M&P students took almost all their lectures and labs together, strong bonds developed among us.[8] I became a close friend of Paul Serson, whose quiet intelligence and devotion to music impressed me deeply. He lived close to the campus in what served as the men's residence of University College, a big Victorian house on 73 St. George Street, where I was a semi-resident. Paul sang in the Hart House Glee Club (as did I) and he was an accomplished violist who introduced me to the chamber music and the Lieder of Brahms and others. Schumann's *'Ich grolle nicht'* was his favorite and I used to like to sing it, with Styra accompanying me on the piano – even as she complained that the text was chauvinistic. Little did I realize how well acquainted I would become with Johannes Brahms some fifty years later!

Traditionally, University College put on an elaborate musical production each year, the UC Follies which spoofed the College and Toronto. It was performed in the Hart House theater and I played flute in the orchestra which was conducted by Paul. The theme of the show was the miraculous teleportation of the college from sub-zero temperature Toronto to a tropical Latino paradise, and it opened with the chorus singing these unforgettable lines: *Now we're assumin' / that the temperature's zoomin'/ it's way up to ninety five / and folks in Toronto / are catchin' onto / Latin American jive.* Needless to say, the show was a great success.

On the night before the final exam in Integral Calculus, at the end of our sophomore year, the great violist William Primrose, Paul's idol, gave a concert in Toronto, and Paul just *had* to go. Instead of cramming for the exam like his classmates, he attended the concert and failed the exam. This meant that he failed the whole year and therefore lost his student draft deferment. Instead of waiting to be called up, he reported to his draft board to volunteer for the army. In the course of being inducted he had to take the army's standard intelligence test and obtained the highest score ever recorded.

To the ever-lasting credit of the Canadian Army Medical Corps, Paul was thereupon rejected, and was told to return to the university.

After he graduated, Paul joined the staff of the Terrestrial Magnetism Division of the Dominion Observatory in Ottawa, and eventually, became its director. But as students, he and I held summer jobs in the Magnetic Division whose mission was to track the meanderings of the magnetic North Pole, then located near Baffin Island, since they reflect the slow viscous flow of Earth's electrically charged molten interior (mostly iron). Today these variations of the Earth's magnetic field are monitored by a network of fixed telemetering stations, but in those days, the magnetic field was measured with portable instruments set up at a network of fixed locations (marked by benchmarks) which were visited every few years.

While I am getting somewhat ahead of myself, this seems a good place to describe my work at the Observatory. Once I had located a magnetic station according to the description provided by previous observers, I set up a tripod directly over the brass benchmark that was usually cemented in a rock outcrop. I then erected a tent to protect the telescope, magnetometers, short-wave radio and chronometer needed to determined the 'true North' from observations of the sun or stars. I also measured the strength and the direction of the magnetic field periodically over several days, for the earth's magnetic field fluctuates continually. Later I used these data to create a map showing the strength and direction of the earth's magnetic field all over Canada, and how the field changes over the years.

The magnetic stations I visited were usually located on federally owned lands and ranged from lighthouse lawns on the Gaspé Peninsula to Indian reservations on the north shore of the St. Lawrence estuary. I traveled in an official Dominion Observatory car and relished this opportunity to get to know some obscure corners of Canada. Once, after setting up on the grounds of a lighthouse on the southerly shore of the St. Lawrence, a class of nine-year-olds and their teacher came by to see what I was doing. I explained why I was there and invited them to come back in the evening when I would let them look at the moon through my telescope. The whole class returned after dark, and were absolutely delighted to view the lunar landscape for the first time.

On another occasion I came to an Indian reservation on the north shore of the St. Lawrence to re-visit a magnetic station. I had trouble finding the benchmark marking the station's precise location and asked the local Indians for help finding it. I showed them what the bronze marker looked like and after a while, one of the volunteers returned carrying a large boulder with the benchmark embedded in it! It was hard to keep a straight face while thanking him. The women on the reservation had taken up vegetable gardening at the urging of the local priest, but they themselves were the only consumers of the vegetables they grew, because the men would have nothing to do with 'rabbit food.' They ate only meat, that they hunted, and salmon which they caught in nets that they set out in the tidal St. Lawrence river. A station on the Gaspé peninsula that I visited was next to a community center where a French-Canadian wedding was in progress. It lasted the whole three days I spent there, and I was invited to take part in the celebration. I joined the wedding guests who sat on benches at long tables and my plate was heaped with food while bottles of rye whiskey circulated at a dizzying rate. Who could ask for a more interesting summer job!

But to return to my days at the university: like most students I worked during our long summer vacations, and by adopting a frugal life style, the summer's earnings were sufficient to cover both my tuition ($200 per year) and my living expenses during the academic year.

At the end of the first year my class shrank to half of its original size, which was the normal rate of attrition for the M&P course. Our syllabus was dominated by courses in classical physics (mechanics, properties of matter, astronomy) as were our laboratory sessions. For example, we spent two terms performing different experiments for determining the two gravitational constants, g and G.[9] That course was supervised by Professor Satterly, a flamboyant and irreverent British wit, best remembered by students of that era for his yearly Liquid Air Lecture which was so popular that students stood in line to be sure to find a seat in large lecture hall, long before the performance began. In the lecture Satterly demonstrated rocketry, a goldfish revived after being frozen stiff, and other wizardry using liquid nitrogen while reciting relevant verses from Genesis and wearing an academic gown along with a steel helmet.

One afternoon, I and my lab partner, Winifred Thomson, the bashful daughter of missionaries in China, performed the famous Cavendish experiment for determining the universal gravitational constant (G) by measuring the force of attraction between a massive lead sphere and a small dumb-bell suspended on a torsion balance equipped with a small mirror. A 'light lever' magnified the deflections of the torsion balance, so that we had to work in a pitch-dark room. After a while, the satyr-like Professor Satterly entered and asked Winifred with a grin: 'Now, Miss Thomson, isn't this the wonderful place for observing the attraction between two bodies?' and mortally embarrassed poor Winifred. Those were more prudish times than today!

Not until our Junior year were we introduced to quantum mechanics, which Schrödinger and Heisenberg had discovered only twenty years earlier. It provided physicists for the first time with a mathematical tool for understanding the world of atoms and molecules. Since quantum mechanics describes the interactions of electrons, atoms, etc. in terms of differential equations, several mathematics courses were devoted to the methods needed to solve them. This was, of course, well before the dawn of the computer age. Today students are able to model the dynamics of very large molecules (e.g. proteins) by using sophisticated software and without recourse to the mathematical techniques that we studied so hard to master.

In spite of the austerity imposed by the war, we enjoyed a rich student life. I played the flute in the university symphony orchestra, sang in a chorus, played soccer for University College, and learned to fence. Occasionally dances took place in Hart House, the lavish student center whose architecture is reminiscent of Cambridge colleges. The use of its excellent facilities (gyms, cafeteria, reading rooms, swimming pool) was restricted to male students. Women were allowed to enter Hart House only to attend dances and other social events.

In the summer following my sophomore year (1944), I had a job working for Hans Lundberg, an eccentric and brilliant Swedish geophysicist whose company assessed the commercial potential of mining claims. He had developed ingenious geophysical techniques to map the rock formations in gold mining claims which were mostly located in the sparsely populated bush country of northern Ontario and Quebec, a favorite haunts of prospectors. I worked alongside a geologist who produced a detailed geological map of each claim, while I mapped the variations of the magnetic field and electrical conductivity in the claim. Ooccasionally, we also 'panned' for gold in brooks running through the claim. To facilitate the mapping, we hired local Indians to cut a series of parallel lines, 3 ft wide and 25 ft apart, through the dense undergrowth; these provided the grid for mapping our data. The line-cutters were paid on Saturday and they usually did not return to work before the following Tuesday or whenever they ran out of money – and liquor.

The bush country around Noranda, Quebec, is dotted with lakes and granite outcrops, and the few inhabitants were mostly miners, lumbermen and prospectors. Towns with a hotel were far apart and could be reached only by driving over rutted, dusty dirt roads or by seaplane. It was therefore more practical to rent a shack near the claim we were working on, instead of staying in a hotel. On one occasion, my partner and I bunked in shack on the shore of a sizable lake, and we engaged the wife of a French-Canadian trapper who lived in a log cabin on the opposite side of the lake to cook breakfast and dinner for us. To reach her cabin we crossed the lake in a canoe in fair weather or foul. That gave me a taste of the existence that Karl May described in the books about the wild West, that I had devoured as a boy in Vienna! The trapper was away, trapping, and his wife, who spoke no English, gave me my first lessons in conversational French (*Donnez moi le beurre, s. v. p.*), but in spite of my long exposure to the language, my pronunciation continues to be a source of amusement for my family.

It was a very hot summer and swarms of bloodthirsty mosquitoes and black flies, the scourge of the north woods, made fieldwork truly miserable in the beginning. These voracious insects covered my hands as I tried to write data in my note book, but curiously, after I had been bitten countless times in the first week or two, my skin lost its appeal to the pesky bugs and they ceased to bother me – an experience shared by other denizens of the bush country. One day, a forest fire swept through a scrubby claim where I was working and I had to scramble as fast as I could, lugging my magnetometer and tripod, to stay ahead of the rapidly advancing flames!

When my partner and I had completed our geological, magnetic and electrical conductivity surveys and prepared contour maps of the claim, we drove to the nearest town (e.g. Noranda) and telephoned Mr. Lundberg in Toronto who then flew up and rented a room in the town's only hotel. Below each window of the upstairs bedrooms of that wooden three-story building hung a coiled rope – your escape route in case of fire. Mr. Lundberg now stuck the contour maps we had prepared onto the walls of the hotel room, and ordered two bottles of whisky. He studied the maps, a glass of whiskey in his hand and used a marker pen to indicate the most promising sites for test drillings with big red X's. His and our work done, and the whiskey bottles emptied, the three of us then headed for the dining room downstairs for a dinner of steak and potatoes.

If the prospects of the mining claim looked promising, Lundberg submitted a positive report to the owners who had ordered the survey – but not before first buying that company's penny stock, shares that rose predictably once Lundberg's report was published in the *Northern Miner* newspaper. His was a fool-proof way of making a lot of money, for the concept of 'insider trading' was unknown in the bush country. At the end of the summer, Mr. Lundberg urged me to stay with him instead of returning to university, promising to make me a millionaire within one year. But I had had my fill of life in the bush country and was able to resist his lucrative offer. Nor was his offer an idle boast, for as I learned many years later, Mr. Lundberg became extremely rich and even donated a geophysics building bearing his name to the University of Toronto.

In September 1944, after I had returned to the Mendels from my summer job, Walter and I decided to make a serious attempt to volunteer for military service. We were rejected by the Royal Canadian Air Force because of our dubious nationality, but the Canadian Army accepted us and we were assigned the regimental numbers B164793 and B164795, respectively. To my distress, I failed my vision test because of shortsightedness, but after using my glasses to memorize the eye chart, I asked to be tested again, and this time, I passed without difficulty. Curiously, the notion that enlisting at the height of the war could lead to mutilation or death, did not seriously cross my mind. Such are the intimations of immortality of youth – besides, hadn't Papa survived his service in World War I? I do recall how proudly I wore my Canadian Army uniform as I walked down Yonge Street shortly after I was inducted – and was snapped by a sidewalk photographer.

IN THE ARMY

In 1944 the war was five years old and seemed far from over. While German armies had suffered their first massive defeats at Stalingrad and in North Africa, their hold on continental Europe was as powerful as ever. The Allies landed in Normandy in June and as they fought their way eastward, the Canadians suffered heavy casualties, especially in the Netherlands. It was therefore not surprising that the army ignored our technical and linguistic qualifications and assigned Walter and me to the Infantry Corps, along with all other recruits.

Following our induction, we were quartered in the so-called Horse Palace in Toronto's exhibition grounds. Sleeping on straw mattresses in horse stalls was reminiscent of the accommodations in my first internment camp, the race track in Brighton. We were issued our uniforms and were indoctrinated in military law and discipline, and what seemed of paramount importance: how to salute properly, and whom. After two weeks we were considered ready for our 'basic training' and received a 36-hour pass, but not before we were so massively vaccinated that I spent the entire leave in bed at the Mendels, nursing a high fever.

Our basic training took place in a camp outside Brantford, Ontario, and lasted six weeks. Walter and I were in the same platoon and lived in an H-hut, so familiar to us from our internment days. The training was designed, as it must have been in all armies throughout history, to instill unquestioning obedience – how else could you expect a person to charge into machine gun fire? That must have been the rationale for the endless hours of close order drilling on the parade ground, a seemingly pointless exercise, yet one that could be peculiarly satisfying when executed with élan. The nightly 'changing-of-the-guard' ceremony with bugle accompaniment, for instance, was evocative of a choreographed ballet. The muscles in my arm still twitch involuntarily, when in my mind's ear, I hear the shouted commands: *Slope - Arms! Present - Arms! For Inspection Port - Arms!* The Brantford camp was close enough to Toronto to let me spend short weekends in our old room at the Mendels, and by hitching a ride on the 'Globe and Mail' delivery truck at 4 a.m. on Monday morning,

I could get back to camp in time for reveille at 6 a.m.

It was only during the next eight weeks of advanced training in Camp Borden, that we learned the practical skills of soldiering and were put into top physical condition.[10] Here everything was done "on the double" and we were toughened in long route marches and overnight bivouacs, sometimes in deep snow and sub-zero temperatures. Although we still spent many hours on the parade ground, we also learned how to differentiate between friendly and enemy tanks and aircraft, practiced bayonet fighting and marksmanship, dug foxholes, and fired mortars, machine guns and a fiendish anti-tank weapon known as PIAF (Projectile Infantry Anti Tank) which had such a powerful recoil that it hurled you back when you fired it. We also learned to 'bowl' hand grenades as you bowl in cricket (in the US army you pitched them like baseballs) and to take a Bren gun apart and re-assemble it while blindfolded. To keep us alert during maneuvers, we were liable to be ambushed and roughed up by members of the so-called 'demonstration team' that wore German uniforms and jumped us when we least suspected it. We crawled through barbed wire entanglements with machine guns firing over our heads and to my surprise I became an expert marksman and was awarded a 'crossed rifles' insignia to wear on my sleeve.

Every Sunday there was 'church parade'. On our first Sunday in Camp Borden the sergeant major informed us on parade that attendance at the service was voluntary and those who did not wish to take part were told to 'fall out' – and were promptly put on latrine duty. Needless to say, everyone got religion on the following Sunday and took part in the service, if not entirely in accord with the chaplain's expectations. When called on to sing the well-known Anglican hymns, the soldiers joined in lustily with words of their own: 'What a friend I have in Jesus' turned into: *'When this bloody war is over / Oh, how happy I will be / No more getting up at daybreak, / No more soldiering for me. / No more church parades on Sunday, /No more asking for a pass, / We will tell the sergeant major, /To shove his passes up his arse!'* The chaplain studiously ignored the lyrics.

Several incidents pop to mind as I write. There was the winter night when I was on guard duty on a bitterly cold night, so cold that you could hear the snow crunching underfoot when you walked. My friend Walter had had a few beers in the 'wet canteen' and on his way 'home' to the barracks he passed my beat, where he challenged me to arrest him because he refused to give the password, giggling while and insisting that I do my duty. Our lives had gone through so many changes in just five years, that this surreal scene enacted on a moonlit road in Camp Borden cracked us up – and still does when I recall it.

Walter Kohn and I have often been told that we resemble each other. Since both our fathers' families came from the same Moravian neighborhood of Göding (now Hodonin), we may well be related. In the army, this resemblance was enhanced by the uniforms and by the Austrian accent we shared, and we were often mistaken for each other. On one occasion, the battalion commander had organized a boxing tournament and Walter, for reasons that utterly escape me, volunteered to take part. He found himself paired with an experienced amateur boxer and took a severe beating in the first round. He was too stubborn to quit and the bout ended when Walter's seconds threw in a towel during the second round. The next morning there was a battalion parade and while inspecting the ranks, the colonel stopped in front of me and barked "Good show, last night, soldier!" Too unnerved to point out his mistake, I shouted back "Thank you, Sir!" I trust that Walter has forgiven me!

Some of our instructors were veterans who had returned from the fighting in France, and their accounts of actions lent poignancy to our training. The 'graduation exercise' of the advanced training course was a 5-mile forced march with full pack and rifle, which had to be completed in less than one hour. A truck followed the company to pick up any stragglers, who would then be obliged to repeat the grueling 8-weeks course. It is interesting that in my experience, no one availed himself of this ready alternative to being shipped overseas.

We were given a final 48-hour leave before our company was shipped overseas. Back in Camp Borden, we were about to climb into the waiting trucks with our kitbag, pack and rifle, when Walter and I were ordered to report to the company commander who informed us that we were to remain behind because we had been designated as 'sensitive' in case of capture.

INFANTRY INSTRUCTOR

After a few days in limbo, Walter and I were ordered to report to the School of Instruction to be trained as infantry instructors. Before graduating each student had to present a lecture on a subject of his choice, and while I have forgotten my own topic, I recall that Walter lectured on the motion of a rod constrained to move within a hemisphere, an abstruse topic in classical mechanics that interested him. He illustrated his talk using a chopstick and our standard issue aluminum washbowl, but left his audience bewildered all the same. Army life had not diminished Walter's devotion to physics and I recall him lying on his upper bunk, surrounded by fifty noisily boisterous fellow soldiers, but wholly absorbed in the mathematical analysis of the 'heavy symmetrical top'. He submitted his contribution on that applied mathematics topic to a journal, and it became his first published paper.

Upon graduating from the School of Instruction I was promoted to the rank of corporal and when I was given a chance to choose a regimental affiliation, I opted for the Queen's Own Rifles – mainly because I liked their dark green forage cap with its red piping and red pompom. For the remainder of the war I trained a succession of platoons in the essential infantry skills, ranging from marksmanship and tank recognition to bayonet fighting. I did not take my responsibility lightly because after completing the course, my charges were shipped straight to the European front.

I lived with the men in each platoon for eight weeks at a time, but enjoyed the luxury of my own little cubicle in the corner of the H-hut, which gave me a measure of much treasured privacy. In my dealings with the men, I tried to strike the delicate balance between a father figure on the one hand, and an authority figure, on the other. The soldiers gave me the nickname Ike, which I took to be an honorific, since I shared it with General Eisenhower. Whenever possible, I used humor in preference to yelling and cursing, particularly, when coaxing the men out of their bunks at reveille. I also gave the men haircuts to save them money.

I was struck by how much the morale and attitude of an entire platoon was affected by one or two dominant personalities among them, so that each platoon developed its own collective personality. Late one evening, a troublemaker refused an order from me and dared me to arrest him. This precipitated a tense scene in the hut, which became even tenser when I ordered two men to escort the culprit to the guardhouse and one of them refused to fall in. I was obliged to arrest him, too, and eventually both men were tried for mutiny and sent to the stockade. After that unpleasantness the platoon became noticeably more docile.

By May 1945 the fighting in Europe was winding down, but the training routine in Camp Borden continued even after Germany's surrender in June 1945, because the war against Japan still raged. My new mission was to train men for fighting in the Pacific. The obstacle course was renamed 'jungle trail' and the toughs in the 'demonstration team' switched from German to Japanese uniforms and sported grotesque buckteeth to achieve greater realism. Rumors circulated in the camp that instead of heading for the Pacific, Canadian troops would be sent to Greece to fight against the Communist partisans in the civil war that had erupted there. That plan was distinctly unpopular among the soldiers and produced dark mutterings about refusing to go.

In the end, nothing came of either scenario. In August, following the nuclear bombing of Hiroshima and Nagasaki, the Japanese surrendered and military discipline began to disintegrate rapidly all over the sprawling Camp Borden. Men showed up on parade wearing bits of civilian clothing, something that would have been unthinkable a week earlier; and in England, Canadian soldiers rioted, as they had also done at the end of WWI.

The army responded to the unrest by processing discharges with remarkable speed. With a small twinge of regret I turned in my Lee-Enfield .303 rifle with its lovely light brown, knurled maple stock, which had been my constant companion for a year. We were allowed to keep our uniforms and greatcoats and that winter, many U of T students could be seen wearing khaki greatcoats or gray RCAF greatcoats. Before being discharged we were given a final medical exam and to my astonishment, I scored a perfect 20/20 on my vision test. One year of outdoor living, away from books, had completely reversed the myopia that had almost kept me from enlisting.

I felt set free once again, this time to return to the familiar and congenial student life I had left behind. And while I savored the freedom of action and the privacy of civilian life, it does not surprise me that many veterans are nostalgic for their military service. The war had given everyone a sense of purpose that helped make the drudgery of army life acceptable, and absolved them from their usual responsibilities. For my part, army service gave me the opportunity of meeting Canadians of many walks of life. The ease with which I had been accepted raised my confidence and made me feel even more at home in Canada.

Hitler, Göring, Göbbels and Himmler, those evil spirits that had held sway over Europe for twelve long years, were dead, and neither the war's horrendous human cost, nor the emerging revelations of the Holocaust, or the new fears spawned by nuclear weapons, could dampen everyone's optimism for the future. Certainly not mine.

NOTES

[1]Infeld once told me he hoped to die on a Sunday in Toronto for death would then be hardly noticeable: Toronto was then still a very conservative and puritanical city. Men and women had to drink their beer in separate bars and all movie theaters were closed on Sunday. Apart from his scientific work, Infeld was also the author of popular books on physics and a moving biography of Galois (*Whom the Gods Love*). I took a course in applied mathematics from him and recall him as a big man, striding in front of the class and endowing his lectures with high drama. He expected students to respect their teachers and when during a lecture, he noticed a student in the back row eating a sandwich, he took him by the scruff of the neck and threw him out of the room.

During the McCarthy era in the 1950s he was accused of harboring communist sympathies because he had resumed professional contacts with his native, now Communist, Poland. He was hounded out of Toronto and accepted a professorship in Cracow, but at a price: he was not allowed to leave Poland again.

[2]My research for *Einstein on the Road* made me aware of the close friendship shared by Einstein and the Mendels in the years when they all lived in Berlin in the years of the Weimar republic. Omama Toni was particularly close to him. She was the widow of Alfred Mendel, a wealthy department store owner and lived in a palatial home in Berlin-Wannsee, which was also the home of Bruno and Hertha and their three children. The grounds also housed Bruno's laboratory where Einstein often visited and offered suggestions. Toni used to go sailing with Einstein and would send her chauffeured car to pick him up to join her for a concert or the theater. The two shared many interests: they read Freud's latest writings together and were deeply involved in the turbulent politics of the Weimar Republic. Both recognized the danger Hitler posed very early and left Germany at the first opportunity.

After Omama Toni died in Oakville in 1956, Hertha, then living in Bussum, Holland, was sent Einstein's letters, according to her son Gerald (2005). When Hertha looked over the letters, she exclaimed: 'Much too personal!' and burned them all.

The last time I saw Omama Toni, she asked me if there were any laws of physics that would be violated by the migration of souls after death. The question had evidently weighed on her mind and she seemed relieved when I told her that I knew of no such laws.

[3] His wife, Lady Simon, was alive and well in Oxford in 1997 when Styra and I visited her there. She was then 100 years old and perfectly lucid. She told us that when they arrived in Oxford in 1934 they had deliberately chosen the large house where we were having tea, because they guessed correctly that many refugees would soon follow them to England and they would need temporary housing.

[4] The Mennonite farmer for whom we worked did not adhere to the sect's austere injunctions, for he had an upright piano in the parlor. After supper we used to gather around it and sang from a songbook we found there. My favorite was Schubert's *'Who is Sylvia, what is she, that all her swains commend her?'* and those summer evenings pop into mind whenever I hear the song. The peach harvest was greatly enlivened by the farmerettes who arrived to pick the fruit while we collected the crates they filled. The constant exposure to peach fuzz made me itch all over and it took several years before I was able to enjoy eating a peach again. As luck would have it, one of my classmates (John Anstee) worked as purser on the steamer that plied between Toronto and Niagara-on-the-Lake and on weekends I got free passage to Toronto and back, in return for taking the passengers' tickets at the gangplank. This farm job was definitely more fun than the one on the Low Farm, barely three years ago!

[5] Students enrolled in honors courses had few options in the courses they took. To remain in them, one had to pass each course with honors, the grade being determined from a single three-hour exam at the end of the academic year. It was therefore something of a shock when, as a graduate student at MIT, I was confronted with *weekly* quizzes!

[6] While working at Bell Labs in the 1960s, Michel studied art history at NYU and wrote the standard work on the artist Wyndham Lewis. He lives now in New Jersey and we see each other occasionally, but we met regularly on New Year's eve, when his wife Harriet prepared a sumptuous meal. Harriet died in 2007 and Walter now lives in Princeton (2013).

[7] At the U of T, as at Oxford or Cambridge, each student was also a member of a College, which was generally affiliated with a particular religion, Trinity College for Anglicans, St. Michael's for Catholics, etc. I was a member of the only non-denominational college, University College (UC). While the various university departments gave specialized courses, the colleges gave the courses in English and in Religious Knowledge, which at UC turned into a course of 'Oriental Literature' and dealt with the Old and New Testaments, the Koran, Buddhism, etc.

[8] There were two women in our M&P class, but most women students were then enrolled in the arts, the social sciences or household science.

[9] To refresh the memory of non-physicists, g is the acceleration due to gravity on the Earth's surface while G, the universal gravitational constant, is a measure of the attractive force (F) between two masses. For masses m and M separated by a distance d, the attractive force is $F = G(mM/d^2)$.

[10] Camp Borden, about 100 miles north of Toronto housed 30,000 soldiers during the war. It was the largest military camp in the British Empire. Armored troops and artillery, as well as infantry trained there and on a peninsula near Meaford on the Georgian Bay, where live ammunition was used on maneuvers.

107

After completing the first year at the U of T, I took a summer job on a farm
in Niagara-on-the-Lake where these farmerettes came to pick peaches.
My attention was however taken up by the farm cat.

At the end of the summer, I joined
the Canadian Infantry Corps and was
photographed by a street photographer
on Yonge Street, proudly displaying my
new uniform.

On leave, with Bernie Baruch in the
driveway of the Mendel home, 1944.

With my buddies,
on training exercises.

Cooking dinner in the snow.
I am 3rd from the right.

My platoon on maneuvres near Meaford, Ontario, at the end of advanced training.
Considering that the temperature was -30° F, we seem relatively undaunted!
I am in the rear, 4th from the right. Note the two Bren guns mounted on snowshoes.

After I was discharged from the army, I returned to the University and am here shown with the M&P physics graduating class of 1947.

As a newly-minted BA in front of University College, 1947.

In the bush country of northern Quebec where I measured the Earth's magnetic field - a splendid summer job with the Dominion Observatory.

5

A SEA VOYAGE

CHIBOUGAMAU AND OTTAWA

After I was discharged from the army in the Fall of 1945, I re-joined the M&P course, after having missed just one academic year. At the end of my junior year, I found a job for the summer months in the Magnetic Division of the Dominion Observatory in Ottawa. My duties consisted of visiting a series of magnetic stations (benchmarks) that were scattered all over Eastern Canada and to determine the magnitude and the direction of the Earth's magnetic field at each of them, as described in the previous chapter. I had a French-Canadian undergraduate student with me as an assistant and we traveled by car along with the instruments needed for our astronomical and magnetic observations. Most of these beautiful instruments are today only found in science museums.

My first task was establishing a new magnetic station in Chibougamau, P.Q., a brand new mining town that had just become accessible by car, thanks to a new 200 mile-long dirt road linking it to Roberval, P.Q. That mining and lumbering town lies on the banks of the vast Lac St. Jean, the headwater of the mighty Saguenay River that flows south into the St. Lawrence. I will re-visit the Saguenay at the end of this chapter.

Accompanied by my assistant, we were among the very first motorists to reach Chibougamau where, we had been told, we would be able to stay in the local hotel. After a jarring ride we arrived at our destination late in the evening, and in pouring rain. The town of Chibougamau turned out to consist of couple of dozen prospector's shacks scattered in the woods, each surrounded by a mound of empty bottles and cans. The hotel, a wooden two-story building – the tallest in town – housed a tavern on the ground floor where just two items were for sale: beer at $1 and whiskey at $10 a bottle – outrageously high prices at that time. More distressing was the news that the hotel had only a single room for rent, and it was permanently occupied by the resident prostitute. She remained for one week at a time, and every Saturday, she was relieved by her successor who arrived from Montreal by seaplane – so that the room was always occupied. (In the more than sixty years that passed since my visit, the town appears to have grown and prospered and it housed 7,500 inhabitants in 2006.)

My assistant and I sat in the tavern and considered sleeping in the car when one of the patrons suggested that we might be able to bunk in the shack of Chibougamau Joe who was sitting at a nearby table. Chibougamau Joe sported a bushy black beard and turned out to be extremely taciturn, but he did agree to put us up for the price of a few beers. We followed him in the dark to his shack where we slept soundly in wooden bunk beds. In the morning, the rain had stopped and we drove to a nearby mining camp where we located a suitable site for our magnetic station at the edge of a large pristinely blue lake. While we were setting up our observatory tent, a mining engineer came by to chat and asked where we were staying. When I told him where we bunked, he commented: "Oh, I didn't know Joe was back." I said that I did not know that he had been away, and was told that Joe had been in prison for murdering his shack mate. When the mining company agreed to let us sleep in one of the huts on site, we returned to "town" and quickly moved out of Chibougamau Joe's home.

When I was not in the 'field,' I worked in the observatory and spent a lot of time at the Sersons' home in Ottawa. I recall with particular pleasure the Sunday pancake breakfasts that lasted into the early afternoon. Sometimes our breakfast morphed into an impromptu canoe trip down the nearby Ottawa River. After 'liberating' some sweet corn from the fields along the riverbank, we would find a suitable clearing beside the river, built a fire and baked the corn cobs in their husks in the hot coals.

On another occasion during those carefree days, Paul, his brother

Harold, and I went on a more ambitious canoe trip north of Ottawa. We spent one memorable week canoeing on Lac Baskatong, the large lake which is the head waters of the Gatineau river, that offered the kind of seclusion we cherished. We camped on a different island each night and never sighted another human being.[1] Each day, when dusk fell, we carefully selected an island with as wide a rocky ledge as possible because it was only on those ledges that one could escape the voracious mosquitoes that inhabited the island's densely wooded interior. The ledges were littered with logs left stranded from logging operations and we used them to build huge bonfires, and when we were in high spirits we constructed catapults that hurled burning logs far out into still, dark lake. Harold had spent a lot of time in the Canadian arctic and told fascinating stories about of the Eskimos' ingenious ways of surviving in their desolate habitat. We traveled without a tent or sleeping bags and used the canoe and ground sheets to construct our nightly shelters. This worked fine, except once, when it rained so heavily that the ground sheet gave way and dumped its gallons of water on us. At each camp site, Harold construct ed an oven from flat rocks in the Eskimo manner and baked bannock in it, a delicious flat bread, which we ate with the bacon, corned beef, baked beans, and the sardines that we brought with us. We slept on the ledges wrapped in blankets, and to ensure sound sleep we concocted a "rock softener" toddy as a nightcap. It was prepared by adding hot water to equal parts of rum, brandy and vodka and it was most efficacious.

* * *

It is easy to understand why I had become deeply attached to my new home, Canada. After fleeing from Austria and being interned in England, I could hardly believe how warmly I was accepted by my Canadians friends. Here I was, a foreigner, a Jew speaking with a Germanic accent, and yet, I cannot recall one instance of personal hostility towards me from fellow students or later, my fellow soldiers or shipmates. The vastness and emptiness of country did the rest and I quickly came to feel myself as a real Canadian. It seemed to me that I had escaped the ancient hatreds that held sway in Europe far more tenaciously than here.

When I returned to Toronto for my senior year, I chose physics and astronomy as my specialties. My summer's earnings together with a monthly allowance of $60 from the Department of Veterans Affairs were sufficient to pay the rent ($10/week) for a garret bedroom that I shared with another student and for my nutritional needs (about $1/day). I completed my undergraduate studies in the spring of 1947 and was awarded a B.A. with First Class Honors in Mathematics and Physics. Having developed a taste for student life, I had no desire to take a job – unlike my class mates – but began my graduate studies at the end of the summer.

During my last undergraduate term, Tuzo Wilson, acclaimed for his contributions to the tectonic theory of the Earth, taught the geophysics course. He was aware of my field experience with the Dominion Observatory and at the end of the term he offered me a summer job. I was to join an arctic expedition on an icebreaker bound for Baffin Island in Canada's far north, where I was to make magnetic and gravitational measurements. As a lusty and unattached 23 year-old, with careers as farmer, dishwasher, lumberjack, prospector, and soldier behind me, I naturally jumped at this opportunity to add arctic explorer to my list occupations.

I had, alas, not counted on my parents' entreaties to celebrate our immediate family's survival of the war and the Holocaust, by visiting them in their new home in Palestine. Air or sea travel was quite beyond my miniscule financial resources, but I heard that one could obtain free passage on a freighter in return for work, and that I might find a ship heading for the Mediterranean by hanging out on the docks in Montreal. Although this mode of travel was clearly fraught with uncertainties, not the least being how to get back to Canada once I reached Palestine, it appealed to me almost as much as the icebreaker expedition to which I had already committed myself.

My friend (and later, my roommate), Mike Beer fortunately helped me out of this dilemma by gladly agreeing to take my place on the Arctic expedition. Professor Wilson approved of my stand-in and I was left free to try my luck as a seafarer. Mike and I had received our B.A. degrees at the same time. He had majored in chemistry, although he would have preferred to study physics, but his father, a Hungarian refugee and himself a chemist, had insisted on Mike studying chemistry. Mike's mother was a fine artist to whom I owe my first set of oil paints. She strongly encouraged me to keep up my art work. Painting with oil and watercolor has been a source of immense gratification for me, ever since. As fate would have it, both Mike and I eventually ended our research careers as biophysicists, he at Johns Hopkins University. His wife Margaret, in spite of being British, was an avid fan of the Baltimore Orioles, and since my wife has been a Yankee fan since birth (she was born in the Bronx), we four occasionally attended Yankees-Orioles games together in Baltimore – an excuse for a weekend re-union of old friends.

GETTING UNDERWAY

But to return to the summer of 1947. Walter Michel, my friend from internment days, was then a physics graduate student at McGill University and lived in a students' commune in a large rented house in Montreal. He arranged for me to stay in a vacant room of the house in return for sharing house expenses and the communal cooking. And so I packed a small bag, took a train to Montreal, and moved in with this congenial group of graduate students, while spending my days in the harbor area, looking for a suitable ship.

On the docks I chatted with stevedores and seamen and asked about ships heading for the Mediterranean. After a few days I learned that the *SS Oceanside*, a 10,000 ton freighter was about to depart for Halifax and several Mediterranean ports. When I visited the offices of the *Oceanside's* shipping company, her captain happened to be present and I was introduced to him with remarkably little fuss. I told him of my parents' wartime experiences and of my wish to pay them a visit in Palestine, then still governed as a British mandate. The captain was a thoughtful intelligent Englishman, given to few unnecessary words and, as I later learned from his steward, someone who suffered badly from ulcers which may explain his perpetual dour exterior. He quickly offered to sign me on as a supernumerary ordinary seaman, i.e. one hired over and above the crew prescribed in the union contract, and at a nominal wage of one dollar for the voyage. He also suggested that I should plan to leave the ship in Cyprus and make my own way from there to Palestine. He could then pick me up again a week later in Haifa, where the *Oceanside* was scheduled to bunker (take on oil) – thereby solving for me the problem of how to return to Canada. This was the only occasion on which the captain spoke to me until he bade me goodbye when I went ashore in Limassol, Cyprus. He was a skipper of the old school, and on board, only the First Mate was permitted to address him. When he was present in the wheelhouse, no one was allowed to speak, except the steersman calling out the compass bearings.

On sailing day, when I came aboard with my kitbag I was astonished to find my Toronto roommate Athol Livingston Wilson, known as Bob, already aboard. I had told him on the phone of finding a berth on the *Oceanside* whereupon he had traveled to Montreal to ask the captain if he could come, too. Bob was a very idiosyncratic and memorable roommate. Whenever I went out on a date, he made a point of admonishing me in a very serious mien to wear clean underwear because 'you meet a better type of girl that way.' He is forever engraved in my memory for playing his 33 rpm records of the Magic Flute so many times that I can still recall every word and note of the opera. A graduate student in mathematics, he was of slight build, mild-mannered and articulate, speaking haltingly and often fastidiously – not exactly the prototypical merchant seaman. He and I were the only two 'supernumeraries' on board and being aware of the bitterness of the recent Canadian seamen's strike, I was concerned that the crew might view us as scabs, but they were, instead, very friendly and quick to accept their quirky new ship mates. The seamen felt responsible for teaching Bob and "Joe", as they called me, the skills of their trade, and also, for protecting us from harm while in foreign ports. They taught us how to make the most important knots, hitches, and splices needed for our work on deck, and while in port, they made sure that we did not go ashore alone after dark – a precaution that made sense to me only after I witnessed the routine mutual hostility between my ship mates and the local trades people in the ports we visited.

The first leg of our journey took us to Halifax in Nova Scotia. It was customary to allow the ship's officers to bring close relatives aboard while the ship was in Canadian territorial waters and several of them took advantage of that privilege and were accompanied by attractive young 'sisters' who shared their cabin. As the Oceanside made her way down the St. Lawrence the deck crew engaged in endless ribaldry about our female passengers. They grumbled that it was bad luck to have women on board, and had to be content with the company of the three cuddly cats that had joined our ship in Montreal.

Steaming down the majestic St. Lawrence we passed freighters from all corners of the world at close quarters, and the seamen found it an amusing pastime to line the railing and yell insults and obscenities at their opposite numbers as the ships passed each other – which were duly returned. British crews were reviled as 'lousy Limeys', but the most poignant epithets were reserved for ships of the Colonial Steamship Line, the only remaining non-union line on the Great Lakes, whose crews worked the traditional 12-hour shifts, rather than the 8-hour shifts on union ships. I did not think it advisable to mention that I was acquainted with Mr. McKellar, the owner of the hated Colonial Steamship Line, for I had dated his daughter Mary. She was a fellow student at the university, and I had even been checked out by her father as a potential son-in-law. While spending a weekend at their palatial home on the shores of Lake Eerie, the occasion felt choreographed for me to pop the question to Mary – but when the chips were down, I had the sense not to go through with it.

My great concern after leaving the dock in Montreal was, whether I would conquer seasickness or be exposed to ridicule by my ship mates? My apprehension was not groundless for I had been sick as a dog on the excursion steamer in the Irish Sea and again, on the *Sobieski* during the first stormy days of our Atlantic crossing. Just as we encountered the first heavy swells in the Bay of St. Lawrence, the Bo'sun took me forward to check on the life vests stored in the anchor locker in the bow. There the ship pitched wildly and the bosun evidently noticed that I was 'turning green at the gills' for he told me, true or not, that though he had been to sea for twenty years he was feeling mighty queasy just now. That comment re-assured me and I did not get seasick until late in our return journey to Canada, when the now empty *Oceanside* encountered a horrendous gale.

The thousand-mile voyage from Montreal to Halifax took the *Oceanside* past Anticosti Island and Cape Breton Island, and we approached Halifax from the east. It was exciting to take part in docking the ship for the first time, and to feel solid ground underfoot again. For me, 'making fast' and 'letting go' was the deck crew's most critical task that had to be deftly executed because a 10,000 ton ship has a lot of momentum. As the ship approached the dock, a crew member tossed a carefully coiled heaving line across the water with élan and precision, to allow somebody on the dock to catch the line and haul in the hawser attached to it, and loop it over a bollard. The ship's steam winches then made taut the four mooring lines, fore and aft, drawing the ship gently alongside the dock.

It was while we were docked in Halifax that I first became aware of the crew's enterprising spirit. They posted notices in the harbor bars announcing a gala party and dance that would take place on board the *Oceanside* on Saturday night, and inviting young ladies to join the festivities. Two or three young women actually fell for this ruse and came aboard. They were ushered into a cabin and plied with beer before they discovered that *this* was the gala dance. In the course of making their escape, a melee broke out and a locked cabin door was somehow smashed with a fire ax. When the captain learned of this the next morning, he was furious, cancelled all shore leave, and docked the entire crew for the expense of repairing the damaged door. The next day a union representative came aboard to lodge a protest, but to no avail.

The Oceanside's mid-ship structure housed the radio room, the galley and the officers' mess and their cabins, beside the bridge. By tradition (or malicious design), the crew's quarters were located below deck in the stern, precisely where the pitching movement was greatest, the ventilation was poor, and where the thumping of the propeller shaft was always heard and felt. The stern deckhouse housed the deck crew mess on the starboard side and the engine crew mess on the port side. These two groups mingled very little and for no apparent reason, there was no love lost between them. The bosun (boatswain) was the foreman of the deck crew, while the donkeyman was in charge of the engine crew; both were responsible for carrying out the watch officers' orders.

At meal times, the second cook brought our food back aft to the messes. Tea and coffee was available in the mess at all times, along with sugar and cans of evaporated milk with two holes punched in the top for pouring; when these became clogged one day, a seaman removed the top and found the inside choked with cockroaches. Agh – the images that stick in your mind!

The *Oceanside* was an oil-fired steamship. Climbing down the steel ladders to the engine room in the ship's bowels gave one an intimation of Dante's inferno. The noise and heat generated by the huge steam engines and the electrical generators was overwhelming, but the engine crew, constantly oiling the machinery's bearings, did not seem to be bothered by this, even though the temperature often exceeded 100 degrees F. The *Oceanside* was one of hundreds of Victory class freighters built during WWII for keeping Britain and the Allied forces supplied. At the end of the war she had been sold to Greek owners with the condition that the ship would remain registered in Canada and sail with a union crew for five years.

In Montreal the *Oceanside's* cavernous four holds were loaded with a mixed cargo: flour in sacks, giant rolls of newsprint, crated machinery, and automobiles. When a hatch could hold no more, it was covered with wooden planks and sealed with a large canvas cover. Its edges were secured by wooden wedges that were driven home with a heavy wooden mallet wielded by our amiable, boisterous carpenter, known as Chippie. All ship's carpenters are known by that name which harks back to times when a hatchet was an important carpentry tool. In the same vein, the ship's radio operator was invariably known as Sparks.

The crew grumbled about the greedy new owners of their ship when a cargo of board lumber arrived that had to be stowed on deck, since all four holds were already full. The lumber was stacked six foot-high all over the decks and the covered hatches and Chippie constructed walkways and steps with crude railings to allow the deck crew to move about the ship on top of the stacked lumber. By good luck, we had fair weather on our eastward crossing; in a storm like the one we encountered on the return voyage, the lumber would most certainly have gone overboard.

AT SEA

One bright summer afternoon, after the despised deck cargo had been lashed down and the officers' sisters had all gone ashore, a pilot came aboard and the *Oceanside* 'was let go.' With her functional and not ungainly lines now disfigured by the stacked lumber on her decks, she made her way through the well protected harbor, out to sea. Until a scant two years ago, Halifax had been the principal staging area for countless convoys that sailed to Britain during the Battle of the Atlantic.

Now the routine of life at sea began. I was assigned to a watch (4 hrs on, 8 hrs off) and took my turn at the wheel on the bridge for the first time. A freighter as large as the *Oceanside* responds to its rudder very slowly (in 1-2 minutes) and it is the helmsman's job to keep the ship from straying as little as possible from her nominal course, at times, in the face of howling winds and towering seas. Standing behind the wheel on the bridge while keeping an eye on the compass and the waves, gives a young man a wonderful sense of power, and steering quickly became my favorite assignment. I also enjoyed the solemn, calm atmosphere on the bridge with just the silent master, the officer of the watch, and the helmsman present: it was a welcome change from the noisy turmoil in the mess back aft.

Usually, there were few contacts between seamen and officers, the bosun being the intermediary, but I soon became friends with the Third Mate who was about the same age as I. When he was on watch, I spent many hours with him on the bridge. He taught me the use of the sextant and every day at local noon, we 'shot' the sun, and with the aid of the ship's chronometer and the Nautical Almanac, we calculated and plotted our position. Using the sun and stars for navigation makes you powerfully aware not only of your location in the Atlantic, but of your position in the solar system, the galaxy, the universe—something today's global positioning devices cannot do! I also have fond memories of the many hours I spent on the flying bridge with the Third Mate, as we gazed out over the dark empty sea all around us and a brilliant starry sky above. That is when he liked to talk about his favorite writer, Jack London, and would recite with rare feeling Robert Service's poem 'The Face on the Bar Room Floor'– in its entirety.

The mess was the social center of the off-duty crew members. These tough seamen from different parts of Canada and Newfoundland (not yet a Canadian province), from England, Poland, and Norway were a chatty and surprisingly sentimental lot, given to talk of their mothers back home. Some were married, but all professed an inability to remain ashore for more than a few weeks – or until the last pay-off was spent. A conventional nine-to-five job ashore had as much appeal for them as doing time in jail. Several of them had been commercial fishermen and it makes me smile to recall the following incident that took place in the mess one day. Two or three seamen were engaged in a boisterous argument concerning the relative merits of red and pink salmon which went a little like this: "I was fuckin' trawlin' for fuckin' salmon long before you whore-mongerin' sons-of-bitches was born, an' I'm tellin' ya . . ." Then, during a momentary lull in this heated discussion, my friend Bob interjected in his soft-spoken halting manner: "There is nothing either good or bad, but thinking makes it so." His comment was greeted with stunned silence.

The seamen liked to recount their exploits in ports they had visited and while these were sometimes of an amorous nature, they were more likely to recall with glee occasions when they had 'wrecked a joint' (bar) in this or that port-of-call. They were particularly sentimental about the colorful episodes that took place in Le Coq d'Or, a notorious seamen's hang-out in Montreal, where the crew promised to take me after our return.

The captain discouraged idleness at sea and when not assigned to the bridge, we were kept busy with chores, such as splicing new cargo slings, hosing down the decks, or 'chipping and painting' which was probably the deck crew's principal occupation. You first chipped out the thick rust blisters in the old paint, using a chipping hammer, then you splashed red lead paint on the exposed steel, and finally repainted the area. It is a noisy and mind-numbing job. At sea, 'chipping and painting' was confined to the superstructure, but as soon as we were in port, wooden stages and paint buckets were lowered over the side and we chipped away at the hull while suspended rather precariously above the water. The rate at which the ship rusted seemed to match the rate at which the crew chipped and painted and once they had worked their way from the bow to the stern, it was time to start at the bow again.

After two weeks of seeing nothing but the sea and the sky, a palpable sense of anticipation swept through the *Oceanside* and before long, we sighted land, a thrill even for this well-traveled crew. As we approached the Strait of Gibraltar, we ran into a dense fog and the visibility was so low that you could not see the ship's bow from the bridge. We had known since leaving Montreal, that the *Oceanside's* radar had broken down on the previous trip, and although rumor had it that it would be repaired in Halifax, the facts were otherwise and we entered the busiest shipping lane in the world in thick fog and without a functioning radar. We traveled at low speed, sounding the foghorn periodically and listening for a response in between. I was dispatched to the bow as a lookout and was peering out into the murky night when suddenly, seemingly less than a couple of hundred feet away, the bright lights of a large passenger ship came into view as it steamed across our bow. I raced aft as fast as I could, yelling 'ship ahead' but the captain had already sighted her and signaled 'full steam astern' to the engine room. Almost immediately, the ship shuddered as the screws churned furiously to slow her while the captain, livid with rage, sent angry radio messages near and far. The passenger ship must surely have carried radar, but was anyone watching the screen or listening to our foghorn? It was a close shave and one not soon forgotten.

––––––––––

PORTS OF CALL

In the morning the fog had lifted and we found ourselves in an entirely new world. We were steaming along the North African coast under a bright blue sky and in brilliant sunshine. The shirts came off our backs for the duration of our stay in the Mediterranean, and we rigged a canvas sunshade over the aft deck. During the night, we passed the bright lights of Algiers as we continued east to Bizerte, the port of Tunis and our first port-of-call.

I could hardly have asked for a more exotic landfall than Bizerte. The climate, the vegetation, the people, and the architecture of the Kasbah were all storybook stuff to one accustomed to European and lately, Canadian environments. For my shipmates the port represented a battlefield, for it became evident that they were on a perpetual war footing with the local Arabs – pronounced *Aye*-rabs by the crew. Being poor but resourceful, the locals missed no opportunity to extract money from these incredibly wealthy seamen. I observed one enterprising and skillful angler in a rowboat as he fished for whatever useful object he could hook through the open portholes of a ship lying at anchor nearby. The seamen naturally frowned on such fishing and showered the miscreant with curses and more tangible missives. On shore, the seamen felt continually cheated in the bars they patronized, possibly with good reason, and on their last night in port, the crew conspired to "wreck the joint" by staging a fight that would escalate to breaking furniture and glassware. I never attended one of these wreckings, but I was given a full account with great relish. The crew's antipathy and suspicion was directed against the Arab businessmen ashore with whom they had dealings and not against the stevedores and trades people who came aboard every day, with whom they were on a friendly footing.

The source of the seamen's extraordinary wealth was their ready access to tax-free cigarettes, which they purchased from the ship's purser at ten cents a pack. American cigarettes were still a precious commodity and the preferred medium of exchange in that part of the world. When taken ashore (after presenting an obligatory pack to the policeman on duty at the gangplank), a pack could be exchanged for a bottle of Cointreau or Benedictine liqueur or the other merchandise available on the dock. Several seamen developed a taste for French liqueurs and would guzzle it from the bottle, as though it was bottled beer. When we left Bizerte I photographed some of these very sick connoisseurs of French cognac, draped over the ship's railing after a last night of merriment. *De gustibus non disputandum.*

When I had studied the Punic wars at school in Vienna, my sympathies had always with the underdog Hannibal. Finding myself now in Bizerte, I realized that ancient Carthage, Rome's great antagonist many centuries ago, could not be far away. Carthage is indeed now a suburb of the modern city of Tunis and after obtaining permission to take the day off 'chipping and painting', Bob and I boarded a bus that took us along a dusty highway to Tunis. Once arrived in that bustling, hot city we were directed to a streetcar that went to Carthage. It was strangely moving to walk among the remarkably well-preserved ruins of the Roman buildings that were erected on the site of that ancient Phoenician city after it had been captured and leveled by Scipio, the victorious general, in 146 BCE. The huge arena, almost a replica of the Coliseum in Rome, was deserted. Since there was no tourism so soon after the war, Bob and I had the site to ourselves and were free to wander and climb about wherever we pleased.

Unloading a ship's cargo was a much slower operation in 1947 than it is in this age of container ships and we remained docked in Bizerte for a week. One evening my shipmates took me ashore for an excursion whose educational value, they promised, was comparable to that of our Carthage excursion, which we had told them about. They were intent on acquainting me in a single night with all three of the Kasbah's renowned brothels, known somewhat unimaginatively, as Number 1, Number 2, and Number 3. Tunisia was at that time still a French possession, garrisoned by the Foreign Legion whose reputation was even lower than that of Canadian merchant seamen. Before we were admitted to Number 1, the madam interviewed us through the peephole in the front door and we had to convince her that we were respectable Canadians, not Legionnaires who were *persona non grata* in her establishment. The establishment occupied a square two-story building that enclosed a spacious courtyard and a balcony that ran around the upper floor of the building with doors that led to the cubicles. It was all very calm and orderly, the madam sat at a desk at the foot of the stairs leading up to the balcony and kept a log. The clients sat at small tables in the courtyard with an outdoor bar and drank beer while a wind-up gramophone provided a serene musical ambience. One could buy drinks for the ladies that had been assembled here from every corner of the Mediterranean and the Near East, but if a client's interest went beyond sharing a drink, the madam provided a key to one of the cubicles for a fee and noted the time in her log. These liaisons clearly called for *caveat emptor* and after we left Bizerte, it turned out that some members of our crew had employed too little *cavere*.

On another evening, the steward of the officers' mess invited me to accompany him and another seaman to the Kasbah and I agreed to come along. He had arranged to meet an Arab 'businessman' at a certain café for the purpose of purchasing of a Luger pistol, a trading opportunity that was a legacy of the *Afrika Korps'* tenure in Bizerte during the war. We walked through dark alleys and found our way to the appointed café where, after several cups of strong Turkish coffee, the businessman revealed that he did not have the Luger with him but that it was with a friend who expected us in another café. We followed him there and soon realized that there was no turning back, for we would never find our way out of this labyrinth. At the second café we drank several more coffees over small talk before the Luger was finally produced. We all stepped out into the alley to examine the pistol and complete the transaction, when, to my amazement, the steward, instead of handing the businessman his money, held him up with his own gun! Well, that gentleman knew that the Luger was not loaded and although the incident cast a certain pall over the transaction, it was eventually treated as 'a little joke.' The steward now confessed that he did not have the money with him, but if the owner of the Luger would accompany us back to the ship, he would produce the cash. Since the Arab businessman was not allowed to come on board, it was agreed that a friend of his on the dock would row him and his Luger to the side of the ship away from the dock, and that we would then lower a line to him and haul him aboard. But as soon as the unfortunate man reached the deck, his gun was taken from him and he was thrown overboard by the steward and his friends. It troubles me still that I had been party to this outrage.

In view of this and similar incidents ashore, it is hardly surprising that by the time the *Oceanside* was unloaded and ready to depart, the dock was lined with irate Arab businessmen cursing our crew. They swore that they would get even with us and that they had sent telegrams to our next port-of-call where their friends would 'take care of us.' The crew did not seem to be unaccustomed to such a discordant farewell and returned the insults with gusto as the *Oceanside* pulled away from the dock – all except those seamen who had been laid low by riotous living in the fleshpots of Bizerte and were now sprawled out on the afterdeck. All in all, the crew felt that their week in Bizerte had been a resounding success!

We sailed East, past Crete and Malta, and a few days later dropped anchor off Limassol on the south coast of Cyprus, then a British-administered island. Since the *Oceanside* was too large to enter the harbor, her derricks were used to unload the cargo onto a parade of lateen-rigged sailing lighters that came alongside,. One of the *Oceanside's* lifeboats was motorized and we used it to get ashore and explore the town whose narrow streets were lined with small shops and cafés that consisted of little more than a few chairs and tables in the street. Greek Cypriote men seemed to sit there all day chatting while they sipped tiny cups of coffee and smoked hookahs.

Early each morning a group of Greek stevedores came aboard to unload the cargo and at noon they sat on the deck and neatly spread their mid-day meal on a piece of paper before them. It consisted typically of a chunk of bread, a tomato, scallions and some olives, the kind of meal that is today considered to be a healthful Mediterranean diet. One day, after the crew had finished lunch, we took the pan with the leftover meat stew to these men and the frenzy with which they devoured it was astonishing! They told us that they had not tasted meat for months.

In accordance with the captain's ingenious plan, this was where I was to take my leave from the ship that had begun to feel like home. But first I had to obtain a visitor's visa for Palestine from the British Governor on Cyprus, and since all government officials had moved from Limassol to their summer residences near Mount Olympus (how appropriately named!), I had to find my way up the steep and rugged 6,000 ft mountain that towers over Limassol. The Greek taxi driver Bob and I hired to take us up the mountain was determined to impress us with his manly driving skill. Ignoring our protests, he careened around the hairpin turns of the narrow road that wound its way up the sheer sides of the mountain. He insisted on having his picture taken with us to ensure that we would never forget that ride. I haven't.

It was by no means certain that I would be issued a visa, for the British mandate in Palestine was in its final months and relations between Jews, Arabs, and the British were extremely tense. But with a visitors' visa stamped into my Canadian passport, I bought passage from Limassol to Haifa on the *Aegean Star*, a small passenger ship that plied the eastern Mediterranean. I must have acquired my sea legs and stomach by then, for after we put to sea, I hardly noticed the ship's motion while most of the other passengers lost their appetite and fled the dining salon. On the first day out, I passed the time pleasantly with an Egyptian dancer returning to Cairo from gigs on Cyprus and in Greece, but our brief liaison came to an abrupt end when she also fell victim to seasickness. The *Aegean Star* docked for several hours in Beirut, but I was not allowed ashore because of the Palestinian visa in my passport. I could only admire the city's shimmering beauty from the ship. I recalled that vision often because a few years later, Lebanon was plunged into a ferocious civil war and the city was all but destroyed.

RE-UNION IN PALESTINE

From Beirut the *Aegean Star* sailed to Haifa and there, on the dock, I was reunited with my parents. So much had happened since we had been separated in Vienna in 1939, that it is hard to believe that only eight years had passed. My parents had already been ordered to report for deportation to Poland (and certain death) when Papa was granted a short reprieve on the basis of a letter of the liquidator (*Abwickler*) of his former business that stated that Papa's help was needed for another two weeks. It was during that fortnight that he and Mutti were able to join a transport that sailed down the Danube to the Black Sea. They eventually reached Palestine after surviving many hardships and dangers, including a shipwreck. (For a fuller account of their escape, see Appendix II.) Not many Viennese Jewish families had been fortunate enough to remain intact in their core, like ours. We told each other of our experiences during the war and they tried to adjust to the metamorphosis which had turned their sheltered 15-year child into a confident citizen of the New World who was quite content to be on his own. Our long and eventful separation had undoubtedly had created a gulf between us that was never to be bridged completely, in spite of honest efforts on both sides in the years to come.

There was a poignant interlude during our brief stay in Haifa. A short walk from the dock and within the harbor district, Papa stopped in front of a ship's chandler's shop owned by none other than *Kapitän* Roth, our old family friend from Vienna. Our two families had met long ago during a summer vacation in Prein a/d Rax, a village in the mountains of Styria.[2] I was about six at the time (1930) and Captain Roth's son, Paul was 11 and gave me rides on his scooter—as he recalled when we saw each other in New York, many years later. Captain Roth had won my admiration when I was a boy on account of his impressive moustache and his nautical background. Ship's captains were, after all, rarities in land-locked Austria, particularly Jewish ones, and he had been an inspiration to me during my emigration years. He had served in the merchant marine, and during WWI, in the Austro-Hungarian navy. After the war he lost his home in Triest and had come to Vienna. There is more about him in Appendix II. More recently, Roth had been in charge of an illegal transport from Vienna to Palestine, similar to the one my parents had been with. Once arrived in Palestine, he fell back on his nautical know-how and opened the ship's chandler's shop where I was delighted to greet him again – this time, as a another seaman.

I spent the next week sightseeing all over Palestine with my parents and visiting relatives and friends who had somehow survived the Holocaust and the war, including Mutti's two brothers, Oswald and Siegfried (Friedl) Lindner. We visited the famous tourist sites in Jerusalem and Bethlehem and enjoyed a wonderful dinner in a Greek-Jewish outdoor restaurant in the old port of Jaffa where the diners danced on the tables to the Greek music. But barbed wire enclaves had already been erected in many places and much of Palestine was effectively already partitioned between Jewish and Arab controlled regions. Both sides were making preparations for the war that erupted as soon as the British army departed, in May 1948. Only a few months after we drove peacefully from Tel-Aviv to Jerusalem, armored supply convoys had to fight their way along the same highway.

Bob had remained on the *Oceanside* until she reached Beirut where he had disembarked and had taken a taxi to Jerusalem – a feat that has not been possible for a long time. That is where my parents and I ran into him by chance while visiting the Church of the Nativity in Bethlehem. He joined our party and together we visited the Wailing Wall, at that time guarded by a single British Palestinian policeman who sat on a chair near the Wall feeding ice cream to a little girl. Since then, the wall has been excavated to a much greater depth, lowering the ground level by some 30 feet. A photo I took of an old lady immersed in prayer at the wall, also shows letters and prayers that devout Jews had crammed into the ancient wall's crevices.

When my 'shore leave' drew to a close, we all returned to Haifa where the *Oceanside* duly arrived to bunker. There on the oil dock, I said an emotional good-bye to my parents with Mutti convinced that she was seeing me for the last time in her life – as convinced then, as on the many subsequent good-byes over the next forty years in Toronto where she and Papa eventually made their last home.

I joined my mates on board but 'letting go' was not without drama. One of the one-inch steel mooring cables became snagged ashore as the *Oceanside* pulled away from the dock, presenting the deck crew with a very dangerous situation. The winch man wisely released the brake and the steel cable spun crazily off the drum, swerved violently across the deck. The deck crew all raced for cover, yelling to me to do the same, for they knew that the cable would soon snap and its ends would whip across the deck with enough force to amputate one's leg. Fortunately the deck was clear when the cable parted and I hoped that my mother, whom I left waving to me on the dock, had not witnessed the frantic scene on board!

Our next and last port-of-call was Alexandria, where the crew anticipated a last wild fling before heading home. In this they were disappointed, however, because the Egyptian authorities claimed that since the *Oceanside* had bunkered in Haifa, where the a plague was said to rage, her crew was quarantined and would not be allowed ashore – a transparent political move to discourage ships from bunkering in Haifa. Or could it be that those irate businessmen we left dockside in Bizerte had something to do with it?

This phony 'quarantine' was enforced with discretion for the ship was soon overrun by Egyptian tradesmen and merchants, ranging from barbers, tailors, and shoemakers to souvenir salesmen. I have a particularly vivid memory of a little Arab boy with a wooden peg leg, who hawked his wares by chanting, over and over again, the unforgettable phrase: *Nasty books and fuck-stories! Nasty books and fuck-stories.* It was the only English he knew. I bought a copy of *Lady Chatterley's Lover* from him, a book that was at that time still banned in North America. It was unfortunately full of misprints because its Swedish type-setters had an only limited knowledge of English.

By far the largest contingent of Egyptians to come aboard the *Oceanside* were a hundred workmen who had been hired to chip and paint the ship from stem to stern (I use the terms literally). They accomplished this feat in just a few days, to the utter delight of the deck crew who foresaw a life of leisure from now on. These Arab laborers were barefoot and dressed in rags and they were constantly verbally abused and beaten with sticks by their brutish overseers. My ship mates were appalled at their treatment and offered them the leftovers from our meals which they gratefully accepted. We were to see more of them than we expected!

Not all of my shipmates were discouraged by the police cordon stationed on the dock. The steward, who had already shown himself to be something of a con artist, went over the side one night and made it into town where he enjoyed a pleasant night, even though he had apparently brought no money. The next morning, several shopkeepers and barkeepers appeared on board, brandishing IOU's signed variously by Winston Churchill, Clark Gable, and the like, while the steward was keeping out of sight below deck. Once the captain discovered who the culprit was, he paid all the IOU's in full and docked the steward's wages.

One evening I joined three seamen in an attempt to go ashore by sliding down a mooring line to the dock. We succeeded in evading the police on the dock and made our way into Alexandria, before we were apprehended and arrested by an army patrol. While they marched us off to jail, a man who spoke English materialized miraculously and informed us that this unpleasantness could be settled amicably if we were to offer a few dollars to the corporal in charge. We quickly agreed to his reasonable suggestion, but explained that we had to go aboard our ship to retrieve the money. The soldiers marched us back to the ship where, as we expected, our escort was not permitted to follow us up the gangplank. Once safely on board, their demands for payment were met with loud guffaws and curses – in the true *Oceanside* tradition!

Once the last of our cargo, mostly huge rolls of newsprint, was unloaded, the *Oceanside* took on an incongruous appearance, for she sat high in the water with a draft of just six feet, and her screws only partly submerged. This did not bode well for her speed at sea or her stability in case we should encounter heavy seas. The ship's owners had been unable to locate a cargo for our return trip and were unwilling to pay for a ballast of sand. The ship did, however, take on board three paying passengers who were bound for Montreal, and on a bright sunny morning, our big, now hollow ship, resplendent in her freshly-painted black hull and her gleaming white superstructure, cast off and sailed west.

HOMEWARD BOUND

Although the crew had searched the ship for stowaways while still tied up in Alexandria, we had been at sea for only a day when three hungry and bedraggled Egyptians appeared on deck. They had been part of the chip-and-paint crew and although they had no idea where the *Oceanside* was heading, or knew where Canada was, they were evidently convinced that any change in their lot was a change for the better. Bringing the stowaways to Canada would cost the ship owners dearly, for they would be responsible for the stowaways' upkeep in jail and their transportation back home. The captain therefore decided to return to Alexandria and to turn the three culprits over to the Egyptian police. The crew conducted another thorough search of all holds, lifeboats, bilges, and lockers, and finding nothing, we left Alexandria for a second time.

We were all the more astonished when after three days at sea, five more stowaways appeared on deck! They asked for food and water and were in much worse shape than the three earlier stowaways. Their hiding place was in the propeller shaft tunnel, the narrow space half-filled with oily bilge water where they were exposed to the deafening rumble of the propeller shaft. Since returning the five to Alexandria would have cost the owners six additional days at sea, the captain this time decided to keep them aboard. They were fed, slept in one of the empty holds, and were put to work doing various chores. Then, after reaching the Strait of Canso, the channel between Nova Scotia and Cape Breton Island, the *Oceanside* was to rendezvous with a sister ship, the SS *Seaside*, bound for the Suez Canal. The stowaways would then be transferred to the *Seaside* by means of a breeches buoy rigged between the two ships, for their return journey to Egypt. In the meantime, the members of the crew collected spare clothing for the five barefoot men dressed in rags, because the weather had turned extremely cold once we left the Mediterranean. Although we could only communicate with them by sign language, it was apparent that these men were better fed, and were treated more humanely on the *Oceanside*, than they had ever been before.

Our freshly painted and overly buoyant ship continued to wind her passage westward across the Atlantic. With no chipping and painting to be done, the crew became increasingly bored. But their boredom was not as great as that suffered by the passengers, for the *Oceanside* offered no recreational facilities of any kind. In desperation, they even begged the bosun to give them some work to do and one passenger made the ill-advised decision to join the crew's nightly Red Dog game. This vicious card game was financed entirely by IOU's since none of the players, except for the passenger, possessed any cash. After a few days, my wily ship mates conspired to cancel all IOU's written to each other and to share the passenger's substantial losses. The passenger, however, got wind of the cabal and announced that he would not honor his IOU's either. Whereupon the steward, who acted as the crew's go-between, informed the passenger that he faced dire consequences in Montreal if he persisted in reneging on his gambling debt.

The weather had been calm and cold since we left Gibraltar behind, but halfway across the Atlantic we ran into heavy seas, and before long, we found ourselves in midst of a full-fledged gale. The ship was tossed about violently by waves that towered as high as her mastheads and they seemed to come from all directions. Because the *Oceanside* was riding so high in the water, her screws were often entirely out of the water for several noisy revolutions of the screws. I spent as much time as possible on the bridge, where the pitching motion was less violent than in the crew's quarters back aft, although the inclinometer showed that the ship was rolling 45 degrees to each side. Huge waves broke over the side and the massive tubular steel masts swayed wildly and seemed ready to snap. Making your way from the crew's quarters to the bridge was a hazardous adventure and was only attempted wearing a life vest and a harness attached to the life-lines stretched fore-and-aft. It did occur to me how utterly useless the life jacket would be, once you had been swept overboard into this mind-boggling maelstrom. We slept, or rather tried to sleep, lashed into our bunks. All attempts to use the galley were abandoned after the cook broke his arm while trying to prepare a hot Sunday meal. We satisfied what little appetite we could muster by passing tins of cold pork and beans around as we sat huddled in the companionway of the aft house. It was scary time for everybody.

The storm continued to rage for days even as we approached the sheltered water of the Strait of Canso, only two miles wide and very deep, where we were to rendezvous with the *Seaside*. The crew was in general agreement that the planned ship-to-ship transfer of the stowaways was impossible under the prevailing conditions. That issue became moot, however, when the captain received a radio signal that the *Seaside* had run aground and had sunk in the storm that still engulfed us. This is how it came about that our five uninvited passengers eventually landed in Canada, and I wish I could report what happened to them after that!

We had just reached the relative calm of the Bay of St. Lawrence when the captain was instructed that the Oceanside was to pick up a cargo in Port Alfred before proceeding to Montreal. Port Alfred is an inland port down-river from Lac St. Jean, the headwaters of the Saguenay River; it is the same region where I had had my encounter with Chibougamau Joe, which opened this chapter. In view of the river's great depth, Port Alfred is accessible to sea-going ships, but apart from that, the town was typical of Quebec's paper, lumber, and mining towns in which all buildings were made of wood, except for the massive stone church.

To reach Port Alfred we sailed up the St. Lawrence and made a right turn into the extraordinarily deep Saguenay river, so deep because it follows a fault in the Earth's crust. The tranquil voyage up the Saguenay was an awe-inspiring experience, the more so, because it contrasted sharply with the violent storm in the Atlantic. I was on the flying bridge all night as we sailed by moonlight up the winding river, its banks rising precipitously on both sides and seemingly only a stone's throw away.

Our crossing had been seriously delayed, first by our encounter with stowaways and then by the storm, and it was late September when we docked in Port Alfred – high time for Bob and me to get back to the university. We asked the captain to discharge us before reaching Montreal and he had no objections. We thanked him for his kindness, said our sad, sentimental good-byes to our shipmates who had become our chums, and took a train back to Toronto – back to what landlubbers suppose is the *real* world.

Ah yes, the passenger whose IOUs were held by the crew, decided that discretion was the better part of valor, and quietly disembarked in Port Alfred.

NOTES

[1] A few years later (1951), when I lived in Ottawa again and worked at the National Research Council, the region, known as 'up the Gatineau', was still largely undeveloped and I was able to rent a two-room log cabin in the woods as a weekend chalet from a local farmer. The rent was $100 per year and the cabin came equipped with its own icehouse where ice harvested from the nearby river was stored under sawdust for use all summer long.

[2] In 1997 Alison and I stayed in the very same 'Oberer Eggl' *Gasthof*, now run by the grandson of the inn-keeper sixty years earlier, when our two families stayed there.

The Oceanside docked in Montreal.

With "Newfie", another seaman, at sea.

Docked in Bizerte and about to go ashore with two seamen.

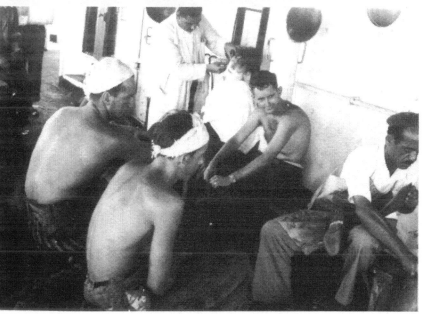

In Alexandria a barber and a shoemaker were plying their trades on board as seamen waited their turn, including Bob Wilson, next to the shoemaker.

Earlier I sat with Papa in front of the house.

There was a big Sabath family meal at Onkel Friedl's house in Tel Aviv.
From Left to Right: Onkel Friedl, his wife Lizzie, my cousin Poldi, his wife,
Papa, I, Mutti, and Tante Pipsi, the wife of Onkel Oswald who took this photo.

At the Wailing Wall an old lady
was deeply absorbed in prayer.
In the crevices of the wall are letters
addressed to God. The Wall has
been excavated by several meters s
ince I took this photo in 1947.

In Alexandria, our last port-of-call, these
rolls of Canadian newsprint, the last
of our cargo, were unloaded and the
Oceanside was riding high in the water.

In Bizerte several of the seamen had
over-indulged and were paying the
price as we put out to sea again.

Back home in Canada, the deck and engine crews, the bosun, the donkeyman, and the cooks, all assembled for a farewell photo. Bob (2nd from right, second row) and I (2nd from left, front) obtained our landing certificates in Port Alfred (below) and headed back to Academia by train.

The first three stowaways, after they were returned to Alexandria.
Far right: An Egyptian policeman.

Imm. 230

CERTIFICATE OF EXAMINATION OF MEMBER OF CREW

DEPARTMENT OF MINES AND RESOURCES

IMMIGRATION BRANCH

Port of *Port Alfred P.Q.*

Sept 26 19*47*

To *Shipping Master*

(Consul or a Shipping Master)

At *Port Alfred*

This is to certify, that *Joseph Eisinger* a member of

the crew of the SS. *Ocean....* which arrived at

this port on the *25th* day of *Sept* 19*47*

has this day been examined by me, in accordance with the provisions of the Immigration Act and is

admitted as a Canadian Citizen

(State whether LANDED or GIVEN TEMPORARY ENTRY and for what purpose)

This Certificate is countersigned and will be surrendered to you by the above named, who is
described as follows:—

Height.................... Weight.................... Colour of Eyes....................

Colour of Hair.................... Complexion.................... Distinctive Marks....................

Dated at the port of *Port Alfred P.Q.*

this *26th* day of *Sept* 19*47*

J. T. Eisinger

(Signature of Member of Crew)

[stamp: CANADA IMMIGRATION SEP 26 1947 QUEBEC P.Q.]

D. Beatt...

Immigration Inspector

*If landed, complete and send in Form Canadian Government Returns.

My discharge and entry certificate as member of the crew

6

APPENDICES

I. PAPA'S MEMOIR

Introductory Comment

I had often asked Papa to write a memoir but he resisted the idea staunchly. Partly, because he did not think that his life was of particular interest, and partly, because he considered that such an undertaking was only appropriate for someone near the end of his life. I had presented him with one of my old hard-cover laboratory note-book, clad in fading blue cotton and inscribed with "Bell Telephone Laboratories", to use in case he was moved to write his life story; when he was ninety, he did.

On the inside cover of the book he wrote a phrase which he never failed to inscribe in his account and order books when he still owned his wondrous business in Vienna: "Cum Deo, 30th Oct. 1973". He wrote in ink and in German, still in possession of his beautiful cursive handwriting of which he had always been justly proud, although it had lost some of its former vigor.

Sadly, the diarist had waited too long. The concentration needed for putting events in chronological order required much effort and Papa filled only six pages of the notebook. In translating them I have tried to preserve his style.

In view of the fullness of Papa's life, his memoir contains few details of his journey from meager beginnings to middle class prosperity, his WWI service at the Russian front, or his perilous escape from the Vienna during WWII (c.f. Appendix II).

Following the Anschluss his life took a dramatic turn, but his spirits did not flag, and with his imperturbable sense of humor intact, he knew that there was just one thing to do: to start over again.

* * *

For several years now I have wanted to begin a diary, but got to it only to day, 30th Oct. 1973. I wonder where to begin, with the most recent past or with the old times which I still remember well: That is the time when I attended the Kindergarten and the public school in Göding, Moravia (1888-1891), along with my brother Max, who was 1½ years younger; and I also attended the 1st grade of the Gymnasium in the Kleine Sperlgasse in Vienna. That is also where my third-oldest sister Mathilde was employed as an accountant with the firm "Deutsch and Sons", but not for long, for she married a certain Max Tannenblatt, who died soon thereafter. She reported to the police as a supposed German national, with German as her mother tongue, but this did not help, for she was Jewish, like her parents, and I too . . . And here I have to add something about my past.

My father's middle finger had been shortened in an operation and this protected him from the military service which threatened him. For that was something which everyone feared, but particularly the Jews, for anti-Semitism existed already. It then got worse but later it improved, particularly in the military, because Jews were needed as administrators and translators. Although my father's middle finger had been shortened as a result of an injury, he told customers who inquired about it, that he had lost it in hand-to-hand combat with an Italian in the year 1856 and his story was widely believed.

In the year 1912 my parents moved to Zistersdorf from Kostel (Podivin), a little town near Lundenburg (Breclav) which housed 2 communities at the time, one Czech and one Jewish, with 2 mayors, one Jewish, often an Eisinger, and one Goyish. Now it has only a single Jewish inhabitant and no Jewish mayor. A few weeks ago my son was there with a cousin of mine, in order to re-erect in the Jewish cemetery the gravestone of my parents that had been overturned. For this purpose he had engaged and paid about 10 helpers.[1] What the place looks like now I do not know, but I am trying to find out and will also try to interest my son in this. While our family was still living in Vienna, there existed a "Society of Kostler", who organized get-togethers 1 - 2 times a year, for instance the "Kostler Ball" in Vienna. Those days are gone and hardly seem likely to return. "Too bad".[2]

In Kostel and in Vienna there were several Josef Eisinger (at least 4 or 5), one of whom is now my son. To distinguish among them, each had a nickname and my father's was "Ruderer". It was so well known that he was sometimes addressed as "Herr Ruderer". One of these Josef Eisingers was mayor of Kostel and another was school principal, in other words, eminent people, and the remaining ones predominantly cattle dealers (for cows).

I want to relate a true episode. One day my father played cards with relatives (or friends) until late into the night. His hostess, "Aunt" Adelheit came into the room and asked with concern "cousin Josef, where are you going to sleep?" and he answered, "Well, I'll see". When it was already very late, he started to undress and lay down in the lady's bed, who had no choice but to find someplace else to sleep; she was, after all, the hostess.

Then the family moved from Kostel to Göding. There I was born in the year 1883 (10 May). Before me was born my sister Rosa in February 1882 and after me in 1884, my brother Max. Earlier in Kostel were born my sister Mathilde in 1872, my brother Wilhelm 1873 (May 27), who became a locomotive engineer, my sister Hanni (Johanna, 1870) and my brother Johann, who in 1891 moved from Göding to Zistersdorf, together with our parents and 6 siblings.[3] There I was registered in the 3rd grade of the public school. After the 4th grade I went into the first grade of the Gymnasium (in Vienna II, Kleine Sperlgasse), from where I was sent to the 3rd grade of the high school in Zistersdorf, as a result of my sister Mathilde's interference. I was transferred in spite of having wept for two whole weeks, begging to be allowed to go on to the third grade at the Gymnasium. But my sister was opposed to it and I had to obey. In this, as in other things, she impeded me in my ambition to get ahead. I was meant to become a cattle dealer like my 2 brothers, but in this she did not succeed, for I became a businessman, and soon an independent one.

First I was an apprentice in the twine store "Singer" in the Westbahnstrasse and before that, for a while, at Paprika Schlesinger's, the shoe store at Walfischgasse 2, where I earned Kr 10.- per month. Eventually I was employed at a sea sponge store at Mariahilferstrasse 97, first at Kr 30.-, soon at Kr 60.- and later, as a traveling salesman with a fixed salary of Kr 100.- plus expenses. Soon after that I had to go into the army for 3 years after which I returned to the firm of Feitler and Co. as traveling salesman.[4] The firm had promised me a partnership when I returned and when they broke their promise, I resigned and established my own sea sponge business on Rennweg 13, at the corner, under the name "Rudolf Eisinger". I was in competition with Feitler & Co. and as a result, that firm soon went out of business. I also had to give up my location when the building I was in was sold. Before long I found space in a building on Hoher Markt No.12 (Ankerhof, Bauernmarkt 20). There I, and I should add my wife, ran a retail shop for perfumes, sponges and chamois. In the *sous-terrain* was the wholesale business for sponges, chamois, etc. with the workshops for washing and cleaning the raw sponges. The best sponges were Greek and Dodecanese and the poorer sponges came from USA (Cuba) in two qualities (Ia and II). In the *sous-terrain* there were furthermore seashells and loofahs in various sizes and of various qualities, for sale, retail and wholesale.

As a further episode I mention that after I began to deal in sponges (I refer of course to natural sea sponges used for bathing, not the edible ones).[5] I had them cleaned and still later, bleached, by the use of sulfuric or hydrochloric acid. For this I had a special workshop where the sponges were washed and bleached, turning the sponges almost bright yellow, but they had to be treated with care to keep them from being "burnt". They remained a "golden yellow" and later I gave them a more yellowish hue to make them more beautiful.

One day, 3 Nazis came into the shop and asked if the shop was Jewish. When I replied yes, they ordered me to get out and to hand over the keys. Before leaving, I asked them if I might not be of assistance to them, since they did not know this line of business, to which they replied "we don't need *you* for that" and with that my business ownership was at an end. The so-called expediter took the keys and as I left the shop he threatened that if I resisted in any way, he could have me sent to "Dachau" (jail).[6]

NOTES

[1] I had taken Papa's cousin Ernst Eisinger, a retired attorney living in Vienna, on a one-day visit to Kostel (ca 1967). The number of men I had "hired", had expanded considerably since I had told Papa about this trip which is described in Appendix 4.

In 1987 the graceful burial chapel at the entrance of the cemetery was dilapidated but still standing, but it has since then been beautifully refurbished (1997). A lone Jewish survivor was then still living in Kostel. He had returned from a concentration camp after the war and had married a local Christian woman. The synagogue and the mikvah had disappeared long ago, purportedly after they were bombed during the war -- an unlikely explanation.

[2] In German: *"Leider"*. With this brief plaintive comment, Papa, who was not given to complaining, expressed his regrets over the loss of his business, but also of the vanished world in which he had felt at home.

[3] Tante Hanni was the only one of Papa's siblings to keep strict orthodox practices, all the others were apostates to a greater or lesser extent, although we did keep a kosher household in Vienna. Papa had an excellent singing voice and his prayers for Shabath and particularly Seders were interspersed by the distinctive lively melodies which came from Kostel and ring hauntingly in my ear. Tante Hanni lived in the Leopoldstadt, traditionally the Jewish quarter in Vienna, and we traveled to her house for the second Seder each year.

[4] Papa spent seven years in the army, three years as a peacetime conscript in a Hungarian regiment (the 18th Field Artillery) and four more during WWI. He was a non-commissioned officer and I remember photos of him in uniform with and a saber at his side and sporting a handlebar mustache. In an action near Przemisl, his horse was shot out from under him and he was wounded in the hand. He told me that his unit's first engagement upon arriving at the Eastern front was with another Austrian unit (friendly fire) and how he survived an artillery bombardment by taking shelter in a latrine. After the *Anschluss* he wore his decorations under his jacket and they may have saved him from arrest when his shop was seized by Nazis during Kristallnacht in November 1938.

[5] In German, *Schwamm* means mushroom, as well as sponge.

[6] The expediter (*Abwickler*) was charged with liquidating the business was generally a well connected Nazi party member. Papa quotes the rude phrase with which the Nazis told him to get lost (*Schaun's doss Sie weiter kummen!*). The Dachau concentration camp was already notorious at the time, although the true dimensions of the Holocaust were not yet known.

Papa was the only one of his six siblings to survive the Holocaust. His brother Max had fallen in WWI -- his name is inscribed in a memorial tablet outside the church in Zistersdorf – and brother Moritz had absconded to America long before WWI with the proceeds from selling a cow he had taken to the market. He was never heard from again and whenever Papa came to visit me in New York, he tried to trace him but without success.

II. ESCAPE FROM VIENNA

An Epilogue to Papa's Memoir

I have long felt the need to add an epilogue to Papa's all-too-brief memoir which ends with the Nazis confiscating his business and robbing him of his livelihood in November 1938. Having successfully spirited both my sister and me to safety in England before war broke out in August 1939, it was his turn and Mutti's to make their escape from Vienna.

In what follows, I have reconstructed their onerous journey down the Danube, through the Black Sea into the Mediterranean which ended with a shipwreck in Haifa, a journey that Papa does not mention in his memoir. This attempt to rectify that omission is based on my parents' recollections as they told them to me in tape-recorded interviews (1966) and in other conversations. I have fleshed out their story by consulting published accounts of the so-called 'illegal' transports to Palestine, foremost among them, William R. Perl's book.[1]

The Illegal Palestine Transports and Eichmann

William Perl, the organizer of the earliest transports was a young resourceful Viennese lawyer, who along with other "Revisionist" Zionists (members of Betar, their youth movement) operated an underground railway from Vienna to Palestine. It was their response to the British policy of severely restricting immigration to Palestine, and their work succeeded in saving thousands of visa-less Jews from certain destruction. The illegal transports began to operate on a small scale even before Hitler's annexation of Austria (*Anschluss, 1938*) and they were initially routed through the (then) Italian port of Fiume and Greece. But obtaining the necessary Italian and Greek transit visas posed enormous difficulties, and to avoid them, later transports traveled by river steamer down the Danube. That route required no transit visas for the refugees because the river had the status of an international waterway. In Romanian river ports, the passengers aboard the river steamers were transferred to sea-going ships that then sailed into the Mediterranean and tried to make a run for the Palestinian coast without being intercepted by the Royal Navy.

While the persecution of Austrian Jews began immediately after the *Anschluss*, the policy of deporting and exterminating them did not begin until September 1939. That is when Reinhard Heydrich, head of Himmler's *Sicherheitsdienst* (he was later assassinated in Bohemia), notified Eichmann that Hitler had ordered the physical destruction of the Jews. Prior to this, Eichmann had encouraged Jewish emigration (after stripping the emigrants of their possessions), a policy that met with limited success because so few countries were willing to accept Jewish refugees. Indeed, inmates of the dreaded Dachau and Buchenwald concentration camps were often released if they could procure a visa to anywhere at all. Palestine, then a British protectorate, was the goal of many, but Britain staunchly opposed additional Jewish immigration, presumably in order to gain the support of Arabs for the war, and exerted strong diplomatic pressure on Greece and Turkey to offer no assistance to illegal immigrants. Britain used more than diplomatic pressure to intercept illegal immigrants, deploying naval forces in the Eastern Mediterranean to intercept would-be illegals. The most egregious example of the fruits of this policy is the sinking of the *Struma* with 767 refugees aboard. Though the vessel was leaking and did not have a functioning engine, Turkish authorities refused to let her stay in port and towed her out into international waters where she exploded and sank with but a single survivor.

Eichmann had joined the Nazi party in 1932 and after undergoing para-military SS training in Germany, he was assigned to the security service. Following the *Anschluss*, he was put in charge of 'cleansing' Vienna of her Jews. His path crossed William Perl's when Perl was arrested and Eichmann interrogated him to obtain information regarding another Viennese Jew who had eluded the Gestapo. While Eichmann was holding a pistol in the small of his back, Perl managed to persuade him that he knew nothing of the other man's whereabouts but that he was in a position to help Eichmann advance his goal of making Vienna *judenrein* (free of Jews). With Eichmann's protection, he would be in a position to transport Jews to Palestine illegally, which would advance Eichmann's mission, while at the same time embarrassing Britain, soon to be at war with Germany. Perl's plan was simple enough: with funds raised from Jewish organizations abroad, his group would charter river boats and transport the refugees down the Danube to a Romanian river port from where sea-going ships would smuggle them into Palestine.

A deal was struck, Perl was released. With the financial support of Zionist organizations and use of incredibly bold and ingenious ruses, he overcame countless obstacles and the illegal transports became reality. They eventually saved the lives of some 40,000 Jews who traveled in sixty different vessels with anywhere from a dozen to several hundred passengers. Not all of them made it to Palestine: some fell into the hands of Nazis and were murdered, some were shipwrecked and drowned, and one ship, the *Constanta* with 350 refugees aboard, was torpedoed and its survivors machine-gunned.

I was first made aware of Perl's remarkable wartime exploits in 1990 by my old friend Paul Roth. He was acquainted with Perl, who was at the time a lawyer in Washington, D.C. Paul and I had known each other since our families spent a summer vacation in the same small hotel in the Austrian Alps, when Paul was eleven, and I was five.[2] Although my tale of my parents' escape has barely begun, I will digress briefly to tell the story of Paul's father, Aladar.

Kapitän Roth

Aladar Roth had made a deep impression on me as a boy, not only because of his stature and his imposing mustache, but because he was universally known as *Kapitän* Roth. He had served in the Austro-Hungarian navy during WWI, before Austria became the small landlocked nation that I grew up in. Aladar was born in the small Hungarian town of Paks on the banks of the Danube, 60 miles down-river from Budapest. Growing up within sight of river traffic on the Danube, the boy was determined to become a seaman. When he was sixteen, he begged his father to let him enroll in the naval academy in Trieste, a plan that Aladar's father, a successful lawyer, strongly opposed. Even though his father went so far as to bribe an official of the academy to reject him, Aladar was accepted and in time he graduated. While serving as boatswain on a passenger ship heading for Alexandria, the steering mechanism failed, and the ship reached port safely thanks a jury-rig that Roth devised. As luck would have it, the owners of the steamship line were on board at the time of this mishap and they were so impressed by Roth's skill that they offered him command of one of their ships. This incident convinced Aladar's father that he had to come terms with his son's maritime aspirations. Together with another lawyer, whose daughter Aladar married, they founded a steamship line and presented it to their two children. When the First World War broke out, the government commandeered their company's three vessels and Roth was commissioned in the Austro-Hungarian navy. In the course of the war, all three ships were sunk by Allied torpedoes, and although Roth was generously compensated for the losses, he invested all of these funds in Austrian war bonds. When the war was lost, the bonds became worthless, Trieste was ceded to Italy, and the Roth family lost its sumptuous home along with their fortune. They moved to a furnished room in Vienna and a few years later our families met.

Returning to the fearful days in Vienna following the *Anschluss*, Perl ran into Aladar Roth on the Ringstrasse sometime after his conversation with Eichmann. He was aware of Roth's maritime background and urged him to take charge of one of the illegal transports. Roth agreed on condition that his son Paul would be included in the very next transport to leave Vienna. The condition was met and Paul's ship successfully eluded the Royal Navy's blockade and landed her passengers on a beach near Tel Aviv. Paul eventually landed in New York where our paths crossed again.

It is easy to see why *Kapitän* Roth had been an inspiration to me at a time when Jews were stereotyped and maligned by the Nazis. I saw him as an example of a Jew who led an unconventional and adventurous life that comforted me during my emigration years when I was, in turn, farmer, dishwasher, lumberjack, carpenter, soldier, and seaman.

A Narrow Escape

To continue the story of my parents' escape from Vienna. Having been relieved of their business, their livelihood, and their possessions, Papa and Mutti received the official order to report for deportation to the 'East' which was, unbeknownst to them and to most of Vienna's Jews, tantamount to being murdered.[3] Papa thereupon approached the *Abwickler*, the liquidator of his business, and asked him for a letter stating that his assistance was needed for the expeditious liquidation of the business. The man responded with: *Ja, warum nicht?* (Well, why not?) and thanks to that letter, his and Mutti's deportation order was postponed by two weeks. It was during that grace period, that Papa managed to secure two places on a river transport which was about to depart from Vienna.

In December 1939, Papa and Mutti embarked on a crowded Danube excursion steamer, amid the taunts and insults of the assembled police, Gestapo, and SS men. The ship got no further than Bratislava, some 50 miles down-river from Vienna and just across the Austrian-Slovakian border, Slovakia being then a Fascist puppet state. When the Danube froze over, all the refugee passengers were interned in an abandoned munitions factory, known as "Patronka," where they were fed by the local Jewish community. They were not allowed to continue their journey until September 1940, when they embarked on a chartered excursion steamer, one of a flotilla of chartered steamers, the *Melk, Schönbrunn, Uranus, and Helios.* These steamers were designed to accommodate 150 vacationers, but on this journey each was crammed with over a thousand desperate men, women, and children. Apart from my parents' party of Viennese Jews, there were aboard Zionist youth groups from Brno, Prague, and Danzig, as well as fifty men who had just been released from the Buchenwald concentration camp. The four ships were appallingly short of food, water and sanitary facilities from the start, and as they made their way down the Danube they were shepherded by motor launches manned by Gestapo men. After traveling hundreds of miles through Hungary and Yugoslavia the flotilla tied up, side-by-side, in the Romanian river port of Giurgiu, about 50 miles south of Bucharest, and still a few hundred miles from the Danube delta and the Black Sea.

Another river steamer, the *Pentscho,* crowded with starving Slovakian Jews, had arrived in Giurgiu earlier and was anchored precisely in the middle of the Danube, straddling the border between Romania and Bulgaria, thereby absolving both countries of any responsibility for the fate of her passengers. The Romanian police, eager to please their German masters, had towed and anchored her there without food or water, and flying a yellow quarantine flag. Some swimmers from the *Pentscho* tried to reach the *Melk* to ask for food, but they were caught and arrested. The passengers on the *Melk* then organized an entertainment for the Romanian police in the hope that this distraction would allow two swimmers with bags of food and water to reach the *Pentscho,* but this attempt was also discovered and foiled. Fortunately the Yugoslav captain of the *Melk,* who sympathized with the refugees helped them to smuggle some food on board the *Pentscho.*[4]

From Giurgiu the refugees continued their voyage to the port of Tulcea in the Danube delta, where three decrepit sea-going freighters, the *Atlantic, Pacific, and Canisbay*, were waiting for them. These barely sea-worthy ships had been acquired in Greece and had been fitted with crude wooden sleeping platforms for their passengers. For the sea voyage before them, the passengers on the *Melk* were transferred to the *Canisbay*, while all others boarded the *Atlantic* and the *Pacific*. After the exhausted passengers had gone to sleep, the *Canisbay* began to take on water and all passengers were evacuated to an old wooden grain storage hut near Tulcea where they dug latrines and remained while their leaking vessel was pumped out and repaired, and for reasons unknown, was renamed *Milos*. Camp life ashore was primitive but provided a welcome break for the refugees after the crowded quarters aboard, for they were able to stretch their limbs and walk about while the doctors and dentists among them were busy attending to the Romanian guards.

This bucolic scene took place on Rosh Hashanah in October of 1940, at the same time that the notorious Fascist Iron Guard led civilian mobs in violent anti-Jewish pogroms elsewhere in Romania. The harassment of the refugees in Tulcea now increased and the authorities demanded that the refugees depart immediately, on the one hand, but on the other, refused to allow their ships to be provisioned with essential fuel and supplies, evidently in an attempt to extort greater profits. The Greek captain of the *Milos*, George by name, traveled to Athens and returned with a crew of six seamen who began to get the ship ready for departure. This is when Berthold Storfer, who had organized the transport that my parents were on, arrived in Tulcea with urgently needed foreign funds just before sailing time. It was too late, however, to hand the money over to the transport leaders and the *Milos* was obliged to depart precipitously, her water tanks almost empty and without sufficient food or coal for the voyage.

Berhold Storfer

Few episodes illustrate better the brutality and banality of the Nazis' murder machinery than the following sidelight on Storfer. The transport assembled by him was the largest, and also the last of the illegal transports to leave Vienna. *Kommerzialrat* Berthold Storfer was a Viennese Jew who had been given unusually wide powers by Eichmann because of his business connections in the Balkans, and his proven organizational talents. Not surprisingly, Perl and the other Zionists who were responsible for all the earlier transports, despised Storfer as a Nazi collaborator.

Some time after the 'Storfer transport' left Vienna, Nazi policy shifted from the expulsion of Jews to their deportation and extermination. Eichmann was entrusted with executing the new policy in Vienna, as he was with the deportation of Hungary's Jews which he engineered with great efficiency two years later. It was Storfer's misfortune that he was arrested by the Gestapo and shipped to Auschwitz while Eichmann, his patron and protector, happened to be away in Hungary. Once Storfer had arrived at the infamous concentration and extermination camp, Storfer begged the camp commandant, Hoess by name, to inform Eichmann of his arrest and whereabouts. It is known from Eichmann's own account that after receiving Hoess' message, he actually travelled to Auschwitz in order to meet with his protégé, the unfortunate Storfer. Upon arriving at the notorious extermination camp, Eichmann could, however, only commiserate with him and he recalled telling him: *Ja, mein lieber guter Storfer, was haben wir denn da für ein Pech gehabt?* (Well, Storfer, my dear old chap, we had a bit of bad luck, eh?), but he was unable to obtain his release because Himmler had given strict orders that no inmate could leave Auschwitz, once he was he was there, presumably to keep secret what was taking place there. Though he was unable to obtain Storfer's release, Eichmann, himself a high-ranking SS Officer *(Obersturmführer)*, wrote out an order that Storfer was to be taken off the hard labor detail and to be assigned the task of sweeping the gravel path in front of the *Kommandatur*. In the performance of that task, he was, moreover, permitted to rest on a bench with his broom whenever he wished. All the same, Storfer was shot soon afterwards.

At Sea

From Tulcea the *Atlantic*, the *Pacific*, and the *Milos* reached the Black Sea by way of the George Canal and headed for Istanbul where they hoped to obtain badly needed provisions. But the Turkish authorities, at the behest of the British, refused them permission to enter any Turkish harbor, and so the *Milos* steamed through the Dardanelles into the Mediterranean and headed for the

Greek islands in the Aegean Sea. By now, moldy ship's biscuits were all that remained of her provisions and drinking water was rationed severely. On the *Pacific* and the *Atlantic,* several persons died and were buried at sea.

The *Milos* was off the island of Lesbos, near the Turkish coast, when a sudden storm erupted and she almost foundered. Her captain sought refuge in the Bay of Sigri at the western tip of the island, although the bay offered little protection. A rowboat from the tiny fishing village of Sigri came close enough to permit shouted communication, but there was no bread or water available in Sigri and the only telephone was out of commission. With all the food gone and the last cigarette smoked, the captain decided to head for Piraeus, the port of Athens. But soon after venturing out of Sigri Bay, the *Milos* was forced back by heavy seas, and with seasickness rampant among her passengers, the *Milos* dropped anchor once again.

The storm finally abated enough to allow the *Milos* to reach the Bay of Salamis, site of the famous Greco-Persian naval battle. Amid brilliant sunshine, the captain hoisted the yellow quarantine flag and sounded the ship's whistle to attract attention. A launch with two Greek officers came out from Piraeus and took one of the passengers ashore so he could telegraph the Jewish Joint Committee in Athens. Soon a tanker brought eagerly awaited fresh water to the *Milos*, along with 900 loaves of fresh bread and several baskets of grapes that went a long way to revive her hungry and dispirited passengers. The Greek authorities, acting humanely throughout, gave permission for the *Milos* to anchor in the nearby harbor of Lavrion where she was provisioned and her large cooking pots were put into operation for the first time since leaving Tulcea. But coal remained unavailable and so it was decided to use the last remaining fuel to make a run for Iraklion (the classical Candia) on the north coast of Crete. There the *Milos* encountered the *Atlantic*, which was completely out of coal and kept her boiler going by burning her passengers' wooden bedsteads.

After the *Milos* dropped anchor in the harbor of Iraklion, the refugees on board could hear marching music ashore: it was played as an act of defiance by the Greeks, in face of Mussolini's declaration of war on Greece and his ultimatum to surrender. (The date was October 27, 1940, six months before the Germans occupied Crete in the first airborne invasion.) The two ships managed to obtain some provisions, but since no coal was available in Crete, it was decided to use the remaining fuel to head for Limassol on the southern coast of Cyprus, some 500 miles to the east.

The ship now reached waters that were patrolled by the Royal Navy, and not wishing to enter the heavily mined harbor of Limassol in the dark, the *Milos* spent the night at anchor. In the morning her boilers were fired up with the last remaining bedsteads, and she entered the harbor, only to receive a chilly welcome from the local British authorities. An officer came aboard and informed the captain that coal could be provided only upon payment in pounds or dollars. Since the refugees possessed neither, they made a collection of wedding rings and offered to make payment in gold. Just then the officer returned and announced that payment had been received and that the ships were free to take on good English hard coal right away. He refused, however, to reveal the source of the money.

The British governor meanwhile sent the Director of Medical Services on board the *Atlantic,* to investigate the conditions aboard. According to his official report the conditions were "indescribably shocking . . .gross overcrowding; standing room only on deck . . . lack of ventilation . . . high risk of epidemic, heavy death toll, as passengers are suffering from exposure and hardship and are emaciated. Case of typhoid developed yesterday . . ."

In the Promised Land

Both the *Milos* and the *Pacific* were quickly coaled and were underway as soon as they were given permission. They headed south-east for the Palestinian coast, some 200 miles away where they hoped to discharge their passengers on a beach, at night. But before long, and in accordance with a well-orchestrated scenario of the British authorities, the ships were intercepted by a British patrol boat. They were boarded and ordered to make for Haifa where they arrived on November 3rd 1940. Overcome with joy at having finally reached the Promised Land, the refugees sang the Hatikvah and danced the hora on the foredeck. They had no inkling of what was in store for them.

The arrival of hundreds of Jewish refugees in Haifa naturally caused great excitement among the Jewish settlers in Palestine, but it turned into outrage when the new arrivals were detained. Two days passed and in spite of all efforts, the British High Commissioner refused permission for the refugees to land, citing as his reason that Nazi agents might be harboring among them -- the same as that used to justify the internment of refugees in England. All 4,000 refugees were being held aboard the two heavily guarded ships anchored in the spacious Haifa harbor. They were circled by police launches to prevent escapes and to prevent any contact with Jewish organizations ashore. Meanwhile, the British Governor of the island colony of Mauritius in the Indian Ocean was ordered to prepare a camp for the passengers aboard the Milos and Pacific.

At the same time, the Jewish workers delivering food to the *Milos* told her passengers that the British planned to transfer them to the *Patria*, a large (11,000 tons), formerly French passenger liner anchored nearby, and that they would be taken to the tropical (and malarial) island of Mauritius, as punishment of the would-be illegal immigrants and as a deterrent to others. The refugees on the *Pacific* were already being transferred to the *Patria* under the pretext that the larger ship served as a provisional quarantine station and using the same ruse, the people on the *Milos* were persuaded to be transferred to the heavily guarded *Patria*. The transport leaders on the *Milos* bid an emotional farewell to her captain, who expected to be arrested momentarily for attempting to run the British blockade.

The passengers of the *Milos* and *Pacific* were re-united on the *Patria* for the first time since leaving Tulcea and exchanged their experiences. The conditions on the *Patria* were again extremely crowded and the food was bad and insufficient. By now the *Atlantic*, the third ship of the flotilla that had left Tulcea together had also been intercepted by the British and was brought to Haifa harbor. Waves of protest against the planned deportations of the refugees swept through the Jewish population but were without effect. Illegal immigration had become a major embarrassment for the British and they were determined to put an end to it, once and for all.

At 9 in the morning on November 25, 1940, the day on which the *Patria* was to depart for Mauritius, the ship was shaken by a tremendous blast and began to list almost immediately. Members of the Jewish underground army Haganah had smuggled explosives aboard and had planted them in the *Patria's* engine room in order to disable the ship's engine, certainly not to sink her. Their action had been coordinated with another Haganah operation, in which the automobile of the British official bringing the deportation order from Jerusalem to Haifa was 'accidentally' disabled when it was hit by a 'careless' truck driver. The police officer at the scene determined that the truck driver carried the license of an Arab who had died four months earlier.

Following the explosion, panic broke out aboard the *Patria*. Many passengers were trapped below deck, and of those on deck, many jumped into the sea where some drowned, while others were injured or killed by cargo that slid off the steeply inclining deck. Some passengers were sucked under as the ship rolled onto its side. All the ships in the harbor lowered their lifeboats, and along with the police boats and other harbor craft their crews saved as many as they could. Numerous selfless acts of heroism, also by British personnel, were reported in the course of these rescue attempts. In all, 257 persons lost their lives, but Rudolf and Grete Eisinger were among those rescued. The British soldiers and police had sealed all harbor entrances and the rescued survivors, many of whom had lost close relatives in the disaster, were now escorted to a well-guarded grain storage shed. From there buses brought them to the Athlit internment camp, which already held 300 Bulgarian Jews whose ship, the *Libertad*, had been intercepted in May.

In 1967, in Toronto, I recorded an interview with my parents – in German, still their most comfortable language – and this is their account of how they were rescued. As luck had it, both were on an outside stairway on the *Patria*'s port side when the blast shook the ship. When the ship began listing to starboard, Papa hung on to the rapidly inclining stairway railing and Mutti hung on to him. Soon others hung on to her and when Mutti could hold on no longer, she and the others slid down the hull into the sea. Mutti managed to remain afloat until a raft came by, but it was already so overloaded that it was barely above water. Its occupants shouted to her that they would surely capsize if she tried to come aboard. Mutti answered that she would merely hold on to the side of the raft and convinced them (without citing Archimedes' Principle) that by remaining submerged, her weight would not be great enough to capsize the raft. She was right and, indeed, they all made it safely to shore.

Meanwhile, Papa continued to cling to the railing until a rescue boat was positioned directly below him, when he let go the railing and slid down the hull into the boat. His trousers were torn, but he never even got wet! Once he was re-united with Mutti on shore, they and the other survivors were taken to the Athlit internment camp.

It is not surprising that strong bonds developed among the refugees who had lived at such close quarters and shared so many hardships. My parents remained friends with several, mostly younger, former shipmates for the rest of their lives.

In the Aftermath of the Sinking

Following the *Patria* disaster, the British administration remained adamant about deporting the rescued refugees. The High Commissioner, Sir Harold MacMichael, insisted that the survivors of the *Patria's* sinking, as well as the passengers on the *Atlantic*, the last of the three ships to reach Haifa, would be transported to Mauritius. Two Dutch ships, the *New Zealand* and the *Van de Witt*, were readied to take them there. At this point, Churchill intervened and overruled General Wavell, the British Middle-Eastern Commander. On December 4, 1940 it was announced that as "an exceptional act of mercy" the survivors of the *Patria* disaster would be released and were permitted to remain in Palestine. But the refugees on the *Atlantic* who had not been transferred to the *Patria* before she sank, would be deported to Mauritius for the duration of the war.

On December 9, a well-rehearsed battle plan of the British police overcame the passive resistance mounted by the interned Jewish refugees, 1,584 in number. They were forced onto the two Dutch passenger ships that brought them to Mauritius. Typhus and malaria on the island claimed the lives of 126 among them, but one month after Germany's surrender in 1945, the surviving refugees were admitted to Palestine – six years after they left Vienna on a river steamer.

Eventually, first my father and later, my mother were released from the Athlit camp, and they began to build new lives in Palestine. Initially they were aided by friends and relatives who had come earlier, for they had lost almost everything except for the clothes they were wearing. Hugo and Lisa Boyko, old friends of our family in Vienna who had emigrated to Palestine before the Anschluss, gave Papa a small loan with which he started the business he knew best: sea sponges. He stored these in the attic of the small apartment building in Tel Aviv where they shared a single large room with Mutti's brother Oswald and his wife, my always cheerful Tante Pipsi. From this room

Papa ran a drastically diminished version of his Viennese business; he imported sponges from the same Greek wholesalers he had dealt with in Vienna and sold them, along with chamois, brushes, and loofahs to retail shops all over Palestine, and after 1948, Israel. He and Mutti assembled the orders in their half of the room and Papa delivered them to his customers, in person. His unfailingly cheerful disposition and integrity stood him in good stead and he was able to repay the Boykos' loan quickly and made a modest living.

* * *

In 1947, when I visited my parents in Tel Aviv, I stayed with them in their communal room and we went on sightseeing trips to Jerusalem, Jaffa, Bethlehem and other sites. It was the last year of British rule and barbed wire barricades surrounded all the strategic locations. My parents were there to witness the emotional creation of the State of Israel in 1948 and the war that broke out immediately afterwards. In 1952 they migrated once again in order to be re-united with Lesley and me in Canada. They lived in Toronto and – you may have guessed it – it didn't take long before Papa was once again importing sponges from Greece, visiting retail shops all over town and delivering the orders in person.

NOTES

[1]My sources for this appendix include: "Operation Action" by William R. Perl, later re-issued as "The Four Front War", (Crown Publishers, New York, 1978 & 1979), a riveting eyewitness account by the chief architect of the transports. Also, "*Die Geschichte der Patria*" by Garson Erich Steiner (Lament, Tel Aviv, 1973) written by a passenger. I have also made use of "*Fluchtwege ins Gelobte Land*" (Flightpaths to the Promised Land) by the historian Gabriele Anderl (Wiener Zeitung - Archiv 01.05.1998) and the transcripts of Eichmann's recorded pre-trial depositions.

[2]Our families met while vacationing at the *Oberer Eggl Gasthof* in Prein an der Rax. The little hotel still exists and was operated by the same family when my daughter Alison and I spent a few days there in 1997. Roth was one of three Jews with commands in the Austrian navy, one an admiral. ("Vienna and its Jews" by George E. Berkley, Abt Books, Cambridge MA, 1988).

[3]While Nazis are well known as killers, they were also very proficient thieves. Only one month after the *Anschluss* all Jews were obliged to fill out a form listing all of their possessions (*Verzeichnis über das*

Vermögen von Juden). I have obtained a copy of the form in which Papa lists his business and personal assets, down to his gold watch chain (20 DM) and his wedding ring (10 DM). I also obtained a copy of Papa's letter to the Property Transfer Office (*Vermögensverkehrsstelle*) written in January 1939, in which he requested that the original form be amended because his business and his car had been confiscated in the meantime.

⁴The *Pentscho* (or *Pencho*), the ancient Italian paddle wheeler *Stefano*, was eventually released and made her way into the Mediterranean. Originally built as a tugboat, she had been re-fitted with a superstructure to accommodate her human cargo, but she was neither river- nor sea-worthy. After the authorities had been bribed, she was permitted to leave Bratislava on May 18, 1940 with 414 Jews aboard. After leaving 100 of them in Bezdan, the Yugoslav port, she reached the Black Sea and eventually the Mediterranean although she was clearly not a sea-worthy vessel. She was intercepted by an Italian torpedo boat in the heavily mined Dodecanese and was escorted to the Italian island of Stampalia (now Astipalia and Greek) where she was allowed to take on supplies. Back at sea she was overtaken by a storm and shipwrecked on an uninhabited rocky island. Her passengers scrambled ashore and survived on snails until their SOS signs finally attracted another Italian warship, which took the ship-wrecked survivors to the island of Rhodes. Rhodes, just off the Turkish coast, was then Italian and was the home of an ancient Jewish community. When it became apparent that the Germans were about to invade all of the eastern Mediterranean islands, the Italian governor of Rhodes transferred the refugees to Italy as "prisoners of war" where they miraculously survived the war and reached Palestine six years after leaving Bratislava.

Sad to say, the Jews of Rhodes who had helped them, fared much worse: they were all deported by the Nazis and were murdered in Auschwitz.

After successfully running the British blockade, the Parita (not to be confused with the Patria) was run aground on a Tel Aviv beach on 8/23/1939. The photo shows her passengers being unloaded as a crowd watches from the beach. This is the way the illegal transports were supposed to work!

The river steamer Pentscho after she was shipwrecked in the Mediterranean. (See Appendix II)

The Patria listing in the harbor of Haifa after she was sabotaged.

The Patria in better days.

Mutti and Papa
following their rescue,
Tel Aviv.

III. THE JEWS OF KOSTEL/PODIVIN

Introduction

When the Jewish community of Kostel, along with all the other Jewish communities in Moravia, was destroyed during the Holocaust, the Nazis stole the torahs and added them to the vast collection of plundered ceremonial vessels and torahs from Moravian synagogues. They intended these items for display in a planned "Museum of a Vanished Race." Jewish scholars were coerced to catalogue these articles. The collection was discovered in Prague after the war and the torahs were brought to England to be distributed to Jewish communities that were in need of a torah.

One of the four torahs taken from the Podivin/Kostel synagogue ended up in the Jewish Renewal congregation Makom Shalom in Chicago (637 S. Dearborn). It found a second home there thanks to the efforts of its rabbi, Allen Secher. After the torah was repaired and it was once again in very good condition, it was re-dedicated at a joyous and free-swinging ceremony on October 25, 1997. Rabbi Secher had found out about my connection to Kostel and invited me to take part in the ceremony and to represent the vanished Jews of Kostel/Podivin. The principal guest of honor was Marketa Parkovska, a lively, cheerful lady who was one of the few survivor of Kostel's Jews. She flew to Chicago from Prague, where she lived, was showered with honors and affection by Secher's congregation. She was made an honorary citizen of the City of Chicago at a reception in Chicago's Cultural Center and the occasion was widely covered by the Chicago press.

All 277 Jews living in Podivin/Kostel during WWII were deported to the Terezin (Theresienstadt) concentration camp on January 27, 1943. With the exception of Marketa Parkovska and three others, they all perished, most of them in Auschwitz. Among them were twenty-two Eisingers.

What follows is a brief history of the Moravian Jews that Rabbi Secher asked me to prepare for the torah re-dedication ceremony in 1997.

Kostel and the Eisingers

Although I was born and grew up in Vienna, a small part of me has always thought of myself as a son of Kostel. The reason is simple: I am a direct descendent of Markus Löbisch, born in Kostel in 1747, who changed his name to Markus Eisinger in 1782. That was the year in which the enlightened Habsburg emperor Josef II emancipated the Moravian Jews and required them to adopt German names. Two years later, Markus and his wife Eleanore had a son whom he named Josef, in honor of the emperor, as did other Jews of that era, I suppose. Markus' great-grandson was Josef (Ruderer) Eisinger, who was my grandfather. That Josef Eisinger was a shoemaker by trade, and if I feel a certain affinity to him, it is because we share both the same name and the same birthday. He, too, was born and died in Kostel, but my father was born in Hodonin/Göding, a few miles from Kostel. Papa spent most of his life in Vienna where he belonged to the "Kostler Club" whose members had roots in Kostel and had migrated to the Austrian capital. The Club's annual Kostler Ball, at which my parents danced till early morning, was the highpoint of their social year.

The little town of Kostel, Czech name Podivin, lies in a grain and wine producing region in the southernmost part of the ancient Margravate of Moravia, about 60 miles due north from Vienna. Moravia is about the size of New Jersey and was a possession of the Austrian emperors for centuries before it became, along with Bohemia and Slovakia, part of Czechoslovakia in 1919. Today it forms together with Bohemia the Czech Republic. In the 18th and 19th centuries there were about seventy Jewish communities in Moravia, ranging in size from a few hundred souls (e.g. Kostel) to about 10,000 in Brno, the capital of Moravia. Until the Holocaust, Jews constituted about 1½ percent of the Moravian population.

I had never visited Kostel while I lived in Vienna but in 1979 when I visited the city, I rented a car and drove there. At that time the region was still under strict Communist rule and any contact with Westerners was frowned upon. The town was then home to a single Jew, one of the few survivors of Kostel's Jewish community. He had returned to Kostel from a concentration camp at the end of WWII. When I arrived in my rental car, I was regarded with suspicion by one and all and could find no-one willing to speak to me in German (I know no Czech). Just before giving up my quest for information, I saw two old ladies sitting on a bench on the side of the road leading out of town. Like the others I had tried to engage in conversation, they also denied knowing any German and as a last resort, I said to them: *Ich heiße Josef Eisinger* (my name is Josef Eisinger), whereupon both women rose from the bench in

165

unison, clapped their hands, and exclaimed: *"An Eisinger san Sie!"* (Oh, you're an Eisinger!) and looked at me as though they had seen a ghost. Their knowledge of German returned instantly and they took me to the Jewish cemetery and introduced me to another *very* old lady who produced a massive iron key to unlock its gate. There were hundreds of grave stones there, some several centuries old, some bearing my name, others the name Hirsch, the maiden name of Marketa Parkovska, the guest of honor at this celebration. Since many of the headstones had been overturned, I told the tavern keeper across the street, Mr. Tanzer, that I would return to Podivin in a few days if he could help me re-erect headstones of my grandparents. With the help of several townspeople who provided the tools and their labor, the stones of Josef and Netty Eisinger were upright again by the end of the afternoon. My helpers would take no money for their hard work but they agreed to share several bottles of excellent Moravian wine with me after we repaired to Mr. Tanzer's establishment across the street.

A brief History of the Jews of Kostel

My father left me a fascinating large volume entitled "The Jews and Jewish Communities of Moravia, Past and Present" (*Die Juden und Judengemeinden Mährens in Vergangenheit und Gegenwart,* ed. H. Gold, Brno 1929) which contains carefully researched historical accounts of Moravia's Jewish communities and that book was invaluable in preparing this brief history of Kostel. I also consulted: Hugo Gold: *Geschichte der Juden in Wien* (Tel Aviv, 1966), Robert S. Wistrich: *The Jews of Vienna in the Age of Franz Joseph* (Oxford Univ. Press, 1989) and other sources.

A thousand years ago Moravia was chiefly inhabited by Slavs and Germans. The earliest mention of Jews living among them appears to be in a document from the year 1067 which required Jews and other merchants to pay a toll for doing business. It is known, however, that Jewish merchants traveled in these parts since Roman times for they often accompanied the Roman legions. Indeed, the name 'Kostel' derives from the Roman *castellum* which was located on the banks of the river *Marus* (Dyje/Thaya). Permanent Jewish settlements (e.g. in Brno/Brünn) probably did not exist in Moravia until the 11th or 12th century.

Beginning in 1096, crusaders perpetrated massacres and forced conversions of Jews in the Rhineland sending many Jewish refugees with German names to Moravia. Once the crusaders reached Moravia, they committed similar atrocities there. In the 13th century the legal status of Jews was that of '*Kammerknechte*' (i.e. indentured servants of the court) and as such they could be bought and sold. Jews were required to purchase residence permits for large sums from the local Duke, although that did not ensure their safety for long. Whenever it was convenient, say, when loans became due, Jews were liable to be expelled and their property seized under some pretext, often for blasphemy or for having caused the plague. Duke Albrecht's IV infamous persecution and expulsion of Jews from Vienna, the so-called *Gesera* (1420-21), is a case in point. Dozens of Jews were burned alive in auto-da-fés held in seven public squares of the city during the Gesera which took place *before* the Spanish inquisition.

There were bright interludes, as well. In 1257, Ottokar II, King of Bohemia and Margrave of Moravia, granted a letter of protection and certain legal rights to Jews; and in 1268, in a gesture unusual for that age, he granted the impoverished Jews of Brno one year of freedom from "*all payments of taxes and from any kind of servitude, so that they may become of use to us sooner.*" He also gave permission to the destitute Jews fleeing famine and persecution in Germany to settle in Moravia – "*[. . .] out of pity for the misery and the need of the Jews.*" But by 1348, Emperor Charles IV, on the instigation of the Church, placed severe new restrictions on Jews and forced men to wear distinctive pointed hats and women to go veiled in public.

The suffering of Jews was particularly severe during the Thirty Years War (1618-1648) when lawless mercenaries of various armies roamed through Moravia and ravaged its towns: in 1647 only four Jews were still living in Kostel but by the year 1673 the municipal register listed nine Jewish families as house owners. While Jewish families were confined to a particular section of the town, there was no fence separating them from their Christian neighbors and the two communities lived at peace with each other most of the time.

The expulsion of Jews from Vienna in 1670 brought a fresh wave of Jewish refugees to Moravia. Some Jews were much sought after by local rulers because their literacy made them useful for trade and as money lenders. At the end of the 18th century, a few wealthy Jews were permitted to reside within the walls of Moravian cities, but all others were allowed to be in a town only during daylight hours and upon payment of a personal toll (*Leibmaut*). Most Jews were therefore obliged to live in small towns and villages where they often earned their livelihood as itinerant peddlers or small tradesmen. A Jewish peddler typically obtained his merchandise on credit for a week and set out from his home on Sunday, carrying his shop on his back. He walked many hours to reach a village where he was a regular, or he visited markets. He slept in a shelter on a bundle of straw, possibly with a pillow and a blanket, and did not return to his family until Thursday or Friday, in time to settle accounts with his merchandise supplier and to celebrate the Sabbath. On the road, he lived on bread, butter and cheese that he carried with him, but for the Sabbath meal, known as the '*Kugel*', there was often meat to supplement the staple diet of beans and potatoes. While life was hard there were also many joyous occasions, as during Jewish holidays or when a wedding or a birth was celebrated – always with gusto. Indeed, if there is anything characteristic of the Kostel Jews that I knew, it was their optimism, their faith in God, their sense of humor, and their love of singing. That ingenuity and diligence were also required to ensure their survival, goes without saying.

In 1763, the staunchly anti-Semitic Empress Maria Theresa issued an edict expelling Jews from all Moravian towns, but apparently not for long. We know this because shortly afterwards, a certain Simcha Chajit donated a parchment scroll and a Haphtarah to the temple in Kostel to commemorate his return "*after having long wandered aimlessly in lands that were not theirs*". Already by 1768, twenty-four Jewish families again owned houses in Kostel, with another twenty Jews living with them. By that time, the winds of the Enlightenment had reached the Habsburg monarchy and in 1782, Emperor Josef II, son of Maria Theresa and brother of the unfortunate Marie Antoinette, emancipated the Jews of Moravia. In accord with his *Toleranzedikt*, Jews were now able to move about more freely, were required to adopt German family names, to attend public schools, and to perform military service. Many more trades were opened up to Jews and the record shows that in 1787, a certain Hirsch Eisinger, possibly an ancestor of mine, was licensed to deal in horseshoes and iron fittings for wagons.

With the end of the Napoleonic wars (1815) the opportunities for the Jews of Kostel improved and as they entered a period of relative prosperity and stability, their numbers expanded to about 400 souls. As elsewhere in Moravia, many dealt in wine, old iron, goose-fat, wool, cattle and horses—the staples of an agricultural society. The 300 year-old synagogue was renovated in 1820 and a bath house (*Mikvah*) was built. In 1870 a burial society (*Chevra-Kadischa*) was founded and the graceful burial chapel was built (see my sketch). The synagogue and bath house are gone, but surprisingly, the chapel still stands today at the cemetery entrance; it was recently renovated as a memorial to the Jews of Kostel who perished in the Holocaust.

On the seamier side, the chronicles of Kostel record a bitter fight that broke out between the civil and religious communities. The controversy was so heated that the Moravian Council appointed a commission in 1888 to settle it. Accordingly, the Mikvah, the burial chapel, the temple and the cemetery were to remain under the jurisdiction of the religious community board (*Kultusgemeinde*), while the hospital and school buildings, comprising three adjacent houses, were to be handed over to the civil board. Beyond that, the religious body was required to pay the considerable sum of 4,338 *Gulden* to its civil counterpart and to contribute certain funds for the operation of the school. This dispute reflects the strains that had developed between the adherents to traditional orthodoxy and progressive Jews who wanted to join the wider society in which they lived. It is a controversy that has caused bitter rifts in Jewish communities since biblical times.

During the 19th century, many young and enterprising Jews from Kostel and other Moravian towns left their homes to seek their fortune elsewhere. In 1857 the Jewish population of Kostel reached a peak of 684 individuals, but by the end of the century it receded to about 400, even though families with 8-10 children were common. The shrinkage was mainly due to migrations to towns. Vienna, only 60 miles to the south, was a powerful magnet and many prominent Viennese Jews had Bohemian or Moravian roots, among them, Gustav Mahler, Arnold Schönberg, Sigmund Freud, and Karl Kraus.

In the First World War, twelve Jews from Kostel died on military service, among them, four Eisingers. After the war, many expatriate Kostlers found themselves living in a drastically shrunken Austrian Republic while their ancestral home was now in a different country, albeit only a few miles from the border. My father and many of his contemporaries settled in Vienna, as business men or professionals. Others settled in one of the many small towns and villages in Lower Austria where they made a modest living as small shopkeepers, cattle dealers or, in the case of my uncle Wilhelm, as a locomotive engineer in Lundenburg (*Breclav*). They rarely returned to Kostel, but did keep in touch with each other. When they met at a Seder celebration or said their after-dinner prayers (*sie haben gebenscht*) at home in Vienna, they did so singing the lusty Kostel melodies with which they had grown up. I still recall those distinctive tunes with fondness.

The horrific Hitler years brought the long history of Kostel as a Jewish community to a sudden and disastrous end and the surviving descendants of the Kostler Jews were scattered in all corners of the world where they grew fresh roots and multiplied. Thus, an Eisinger family reunion in London in 1994 brought together relatives who lived in the United States, Australia, England, Canada, Spain, Israel and Austria! And so it seems only fitting that the torah that once resided in Kostel should also have found a new home in the New World!

IV. PHYSICS AND BEYOND

A brief scientific *curriculum vitae*

Although this little book is primarily a memoir of my youthful years, I have been persuaded to add a brief account of my subsequent experiences as a research scientist.

I was originally drawn to physics because it offered a haven of rationality at a time when I had little faith in politics, religion, or philosophy as guides. Victor Weisskopf, who was one of my professors at MIT, titled his autobiography *The Joys of Insight* and that phrase captures the satisfaction I derive from physics – from the quest to understand how the universe works. In my later years I found a similar satisfaction from my research in molecular biology, history, and biography – human society being, ultimately, a manifestation of the laws of nature.

My research career ran concurrently with the great advances in physics that took place beginning with the twentieth century, advances that in turn spawned the technologies that have profoundly changed human society and are continuing to do so. My own research work began in nuclear physics, gradually shifted to molecular biology and medicine and eventually ended up in history and biography. This brief account of my journey is not intended to draw attention to my modest contributions, but to provide a few sign posts in the professional life of this 'journeyman physicist.'

* * *

Students enrolled in the Mathematics and Physics honor course (known as M&P) at the University of Toronto devoted the first two years to the study of classical physics (mechanics, optics, electro-magnetism) and calculus (differential and integral). We were not introduced to quantum mechanics until our third year. Apart from attending lectures, we spent some ten hours a week in the laboratory where we performed classical physics experiments and wrote detailed reports about them. I still possess a couple of my old lab notebooks and am amazed at their erudition! At the end of each academic year, we had to pass a three-hour-long exam in each of our courses to be allowed to continue.

In astronomy, my 'minor' subject, we used 10-place logarithmic tables, bound in heavy tomes, for our astronomical calculations – calculations that today's smallest computer would perform in a flash. Our entire third-year physics lab was devoted to determining the two gravitational constants, using several different experimental methods – Newton and gravity ruled supreme. The emphasis was on identifying every potential source of experimental error, and this kind of error analysis became habitual in my future research work.

For my Master's thesis I employed an elegant spectroscopic technique (Raman spectroscopy) to investigate how the rotation of (CH_4) molecules is affected by increasing gas pressure, and hence, by the collision rate of the molecules. Methane gas in a specially designed high pressure 'Raman tube' was irradiated by light from two powerful mercury arc lamps and the light scattered by the CH_4 molecules was analyzed using a high-resolution spectrograph. The spectra were recorded photographically and revealed how increasing the gas pressure perturbed the rotation of the CH_4 molecules – not a breath-taking finding, but my first semi-independent research project all the same.

Spectroscopy would become an important part of my scientific bag of tricks and I used various spectroscopic techniques to investigate systems ranging from atomic nuclei and biological molecules, to cell membranes and red blood cells.

In 1948, I was awarded a teaching fellowship at MIT, thanks to a recommendation of Professor Harry Welsh. I moved to Cambridge and enrolled as a graduate student in Course 8 (Physics) of that admirable institution. After Toronto, Cambridge provided a tremendously more stimulating environment – in its cultural and social life, as well as in physics. I took courses in the theory of functions (math), in quantum mechanics, and in nuclear physics, and audited the lectures of the renowned Julian Schwinger at Harvard, up the Charles River from MIT. At the end of my first year, I joined the 'atomic beam lab' of Professor Jerrold Zacharias and three years later, was awarded my PhD for determining the quantum states of the protons and neutrons inside the nucleus, and how they interact with each other.

The atomic beam lab was housed in Building 20, a "temporary" wooden structure built during WWII for radar-related research and not demolished until 2000. The lab was staffed with 4-5 graduate students working on their thesis problems and by three technicians, who helped the students build their experimental equipment in a substantial machine shop.

The following brief description of a typical atomic beam experiment illustrates its complexity: Inside a 10 ft-long, 15 inch-diameter cast-brass vacuum chamber (known as the "can") a stream of potassium (K) atoms issued from a slit in small oven located at one end of the can. The stream of atoms was collimated by slits and traveled to a detector at the far end of the can. Their trajectory was determined by the constant magnetic and electro-magnetic fields they passed through. Their trajectory could be altered by tuning the electro-magnetic field to a frequency which changed an atom's magnetic quantum state. This, in turn, affected the atoms' trajectory and hence the rate at which they arrived at the detector at the far end of the can. The detector (a hot tungsten wire) ionized each arriving K atom whereupon the charged K^+ ions were accelerated in an electric field before entering a mass spectrometer that separated the three potassium isotopes. Upon entering the electron-multiplier an arriving ion generated an avalanche of electrons which activated a loud-speaker which announced the arrival of each atom at the detector with a click. The experimenter listened to the click rate while tuning the radio-frequency field to determines the frequencies (energies) at which the atoms undergo transitions.

To prevent the atoms in the beam from being scattered by residual air molecules, an exquisitely high vacuum had to be maintained inside the can – less than a trillionth of atmospheric pressure. To achieve it the can was continuously evacuated by several mercury diffusion pumps, but since tiny leaks were unavoidable, the experimenter had to spend many hours during many nights searching for leaks with a special leak detector and sealing them when he found one. It was indeed so rare that all components of this elaborate apparatus functioned at the same time, that we graduate students had the motto: "Never leave a running apparatus!" After two years of constructing and testing the apparatus, I was able to collect all the data I needed for my thesis in just a few days. My results confirmed a particular model for the interior structure of the nucleus that had been proposed by Aage Bohr (Niels's son) and Ben Mottelson: Neutrons and protons, separately, occupy quantized states and shells, much as do the electrons of an atom. (This orderly model of the nucleus was subsequently greatly complicated by the discovery of additional elementary particles.)

Such sophisticated atomic beam experiments are descendants of the classic Stern-Gerlach experiment (1922) that demonstrated for the first time that atomic electrons have spin with two magnetic quantum states. It is interesting that my thesis supervisor, Jerrold Zacharias, had been a student of I. I. Rabi, who had been a student of Otto Stern. This is typical of the way "tricks of the trade" were passed on to succeeding generations of experimenters!

Nuclear physics was at center stage in those days and funds for research seemed inexhaustible. Physicists who had worked on the Manhattan Project during the war, returned to universities and adapted the new technologies developed there to fundamental physics research. At MIT, the 320 Mev synchrotron had just been completed and was capable of generating very high energy photons. After I finished my thesis, I used these photons to study the photo-nuclear reactions they initiated when they bombarded various target nuclei – another approach to investigating the interior structure of nuclei. At about that time, Tom Bonner, chairman of the Physics Department at Rice University visited MIT and offered me a post-doc position. I was to pursue similar experiments, using the new 20 Mev Van de Graaf (electro-static) accelerator that Bonner had just ordered.

I accepted his offer, but having entered the U.S. as a student, I had to return to Canada in order to obtain a U.S. immigration visa. Because this happened at the height of the McCarthy era of paranoia (1952) when atomic spies were thought to be lurking everywhere, it took a year before my visa was finally approved. While waiting for my visa, I was fortunate to get interesting temporary jobs, first at the Dominion Observatory where I plotted the movements of Earth's shifting magnetic pole; and later, and at the National Research Council of Canada where I investigated the interior structure of chromium nuclei in an atomic beam experiment in which I collaborated with Peter Brix, a visiting German physicist who became a good friend whom I often visited in Heidelberg in the years to come.

The Van de Graaf accelerator arrived at Rice at about the same time as I. Along with three other post-docs, we accelerated protons and deuterons and bombarded various target nuclei with them. By identifying the products of the resulting reactions, and by measuring their energy and angular distributions, we characterized the excited states of the target nuclei. Being brand-new, the accelerator was, unfortunately, beset by 'bugs' and it took many weeks and many nights of hard work before the accelerator functioned stably enough for our experiments.

While I was at Rice University, the physics department hosted a conference on low-temperature physics, and Arthur Schawlow, who had been a fellow student in Toronto, was among the participants. Arthur was a New Orleans jazz enthusiast and asked me where one could hear good live jazz in Houston. My inquiries led to a small 'strip club', said to have the best jazz combo, and one afternoon, Arthur and I skipped the talks and went there to check it out. When we arrived, we noticed that the strippers seemed to perform for a particular customer sitting at the end of the little runway. That customer turned out to be Richard Feynman who had also skipped the afternoon session. We joined him and spent a most enjoyable afternoon in his company. Feynman, recognized as probably the most brilliant theoretical physicist of that era, had such an open and unaffected manner towards everyone he met that by the time we joined him, he had charmed all the performers and knew all their names. As it happens, both Feynman and Schawlow were awarded Nobel prizes shortly afterwards.

Because the complexity and the cost of instrumentation of nuclear research required ever larger teams of physicists, this style of performing research did not appeal to me in the long run. Although I lived luxuriously next to a bayou, in the home of Adrienne Audrey (Tom and Jara Bonner's good friend), I found Houston's social and intellectual life in the 1950s to be bland, its climate appalling, and its flat topography unappealing. I was therefore thrilled when Sidney Millman, himself a former atomic beamer, and now director of physics research at Bell Labs, approached me during a meeting of the American Physical Society in New York and invited to an interview at the Labs. The prospect of returning to the East delighted me. A few weeks later, I was invited to present a seminar about my research at the Labs and after surviving two-days of intense interviews with a dozen of the resident scientists, I was offered a position in the basic research area of Bell Labs in Murray Hill, New Jersey.

Bell Labs was then among the foremost research laboratories anywhere and its scientists were responsible for many fundamental discoveries and inventions, including transistors, lasers, LEDs, CCDs, cellular phones, integrated circuits, and software, inventions and technologies that are changing society profoundly. AT&T's anti-trust agreement with the government obliged the company to make all Bell Labs patents freely available to the public, in return for being permitted to retain its monopoly of the telephone system. As others exploited these technologies, AT&T's monopoly was challenged and eventually this led to the dismemberment of the company, and to the demise of Bell Labs and its liberal research policy. But this was still thirty years in the future.

Before starting to work at Bell Labs, I requested and received three months leave of absence to allow me to return to Europe for the first time since the war. Since I was single with my nomadic instinct very much intact, I bought a motorcycle in Glasgow, drove on it through France and the Alps to Rome, and from there to Venice. There I stored the motorcycle and took a boat to Greece, and from there, to Constantinople. I returned to Venice on the Orient Express, picked up my bike, and rode it to Bremen; from there it was shipped to Newark while I flew back to New York.

Back in Murray Hill, I was assigned a laboratory and an office, hired a research assistant, and had seemingly unlimited funds for equipment at my disposal. I was free to work on anything of scientific interest – a freedom granted to the few hundred members of the basic research area, which constituted about ten percent of Bell Labs. The remainder of Bell Labs was devoted to applied research, e.g. the development of trans-Atlantic cables (then still equipped with vacuum tube amplifiers!), or improving telephones and switches – the life blood of AT&T's vast telephone system. The long corridors of the Murray Hill building in which I worked, housed theoretical and experimental scientists with expertise in many different fields, and all were ready to chat or to collaborate with you in a collegial and non-competitive atmosphere. Numerous seminars, visiting academics, and excellent library facilities allowed one to stay in touch with the latest developments in science, as well as at a university.

At the Labs, I found a close friend in George Feher, a solid-state physicist and a *Landsmann* from Bratislava who had arrived at the Labs via Israel and Berkeley, California. George developed a novel microwave technique (ENDOR) with which transitions between the magnetic states of atoms could be observed while the atoms were imbedded in a silicon crystal. I recognized that with ENDOR one could investigate nuclei in much the same way as in atomic beam experiments. To demonstrate this, George and I used the technique to discover the structure of two antimony nuclei – but this was my last foray into nuclear structures. Before leaving that field, I and Vincent Jaccarino co-authored a review of that topic for the Reviews of Modern Physics. Vince had been a fellow student at MIT and we used to go sketching together on Cape Anne.

In 1953 Watson and Crick discovered the double helical structure of DNA and in the years that followed, Crick unraveled the molecular mechanism which uses the DNA's genetic information to synthesize proteins. The importance of these discoveries rippled through the scientific community and many physicists were attracted to the emergent field of molecular biology. Physicists at Bell Labs were no exception and three of us (W. E. Blumberg. R. G. Shulman, and I) proposed the formation of a molecular biophysics department at Bell Labs, which duly became a reality. Our research now shifted from pure physics to employing the physicist's tools (e.g. emission spectroscopy, nuclear magnetic resonance) to study biological systems on the molecular level. This shift obliged me to become knowledgeable in biochemistry, a subject I had never studied. I embarked on a study of the excited states of nucleic acids and proteins and on the basis of that research, I won a Guggenheim Fellowship that allowed our family to spend a year in Europe, where I acquired the basic skills of microbiology in the laboratories of Ole Maaloe (University of Copenhagen) and Alfred Tissiéres (University of Geneva). I cannot resist injecting that Alfred was an experienced Alpinist and together with him, I climbed the Pigne d'Arolla in the Swiss Alps a few years later, in 1966. During our descent I fell into a crevasse and Alfred, to whom I was fortunately belayed, hauled me out.

After my return to Bell Labs began a very productive period – in terms of the number of publications. I investigated the molecular damage that radiation produces in DNA molecules – an issue that was deemed to be of great importance at a time when memories of the Hiroshima and Nagasaki bombs were still fresh. Our group used spectroscopic and magnetic resonance techniques for studying radiation damage in biological molecules, particularly DNA, and we organized a big international conference devoted to Biological Molecules in their Excited States which attracted scientists from many countries. Soon after it was over, however, Richard and Jane Setlow made a remarkable discovery: in the living cell, DNA is always accompanied by a group of specialized enzymes that repair any damage in one DNA strand, quickly and precisely, by employing the (undamaged) complementary strand as a template. Not surprisingly, interest in the field of DNA damage faded following the discovery of these repair enzymes and I turned to other areas of molecular biology.

In 1960 my colleagues and I studied the binding of metal ions to DNA and discovered, somewhat serendipitously, that when paramagnetic ions (e.g. Mn^{2+}) bind to DNA, the magnetic relaxation time of the solvent water is shortened dramatically. We named the phenomenon 'proton relaxation enhancement' (or PRE) and studied it in detail, as did other researchers. The deeper understanding of PRE led to the development of different PRE probes which are widely used for enhancing medical imaging (MRI). I also developed a spectroscopic technique with which I showed how codons recognizes their specific transfer-RNAs, an important step in protein synthesis – at the time still a hot topic in molecular biology. (The codon is the trinucleotide that calls for the insertion of a specific amino acid in the nascent protein.)

In the 1970s I became interested in an obscure quantum mechanics phenomenon, known as 'resonance energy transfer' (RET or FRET). In FRET the energy of an "excited" molecule (the donor) is spontaneously transferred to a suitable acceptor molecule (the acceptor) – without any radiation (photons) being emitted or absorbed. Because the rate at which the energy transfer occurs depends strongly on the separation between donor and acceptor, the rate of FRET can be used to determine the distance between labeled molecular sites – a useful piece of information for scientists studying the conformation of proteins and other biological molecules.

Together with my English friend and post-doc, Bob Dale, we validated the FRET technique, both by developing its theory and by experiments. We then used it to obtain certain structural parameters for hormones, proteins, RNA molecules, even red blood cells. FRET continues to be a widely used technique in molecular biology and I recently discovered that our FRET papers are the most frequently cited ones of all my publications. While we were heavily engaged in this work, Bob often stayed overnight with our family in Cleehill where he was always a welcome guest. He excelled at telling frightful ghostly bedtime stories to Alison and Simon, then about seven and five, as they lay spellbound in their double-decker bunk beds.

With the help of the excellent machine and glass blowing shops of Bell Labs I was able to develop some novel experimental techniques, e.g. 'quantitative gel chromatography' for studying binding to macromolecules and 'front-face fluorometry' which became the basis of a practical diagnostic device, the hematofluorometer. My colleagues (Blumberg and Lamola) and I were awarded a patent for it and we demonstrated its efficacy for diagnosing a several different clinical conditions, including porphyrias and bilirubinemia. But its most important application was the ZPP-hematofluorometer, a portable instrument which employs a single drop of blood (obtained by finger stick) to obtain a quantitative assay of a subject's past lead exposure. The instrument made it feasible to screen subjects for lead exposure more quickly and more cheaply than by existing methods. Together with Irving Selikoff's renowned occupational medicine group at the Mount Sinai School of Medicine, we demonstrated the hematofluorometer's efficacy in several epidemiological studies of lead-exposed populations. Our data documented the deleterious health effects of lead in populations ranging from pre-school children to demolition workers, as well as in the general public. We were invited to present our results at governmental hearings in Washington and they played an important role in passing legislation that banned leaded gasoline (1995), as well as lead-based paints – not, incidentally, without powerful objections raised by industrial and oil corporations.

My work with the Selikoff's group of physicians made me aware of subtleties of lead disease, its long and disastrous history, and of the history of medicine in general.[1] After writing a few short pieces that chronicled the numerous epidemic outbreaks of plumbism since antiquity, I won a (second) Guggenheim fellowship in 1977 which allowed me to extend my historical research. Bell Labs granted me a sabbatical leave, albeit somewhat reluctantly, and our little family moved to Cambridge for a year. My old friend Martin Ostwald (then classics professor at Swarthmore, and many years ago, my Latin tutor when we were fellow-internees) introduced me to Moses Finley, an eminent classics scholar and Master of Darwin College, who appointed me Visiting Fellow of the College. I recall with pleasure our philosophical pre-luncheon conversations over glasses of whiskey in his study at the College. Styra and I rented a small house in Girton where Alison and Simon (9 and

11 at the time) had the memorable experience of attending an English public school, while Styra embarked on her first musicological research project.

By scouring the libraries of Cambridge University and the Wellcome Foundation in London I learned of the frequent, often fatal, outbreaks of the *colica Pictonum*, a debilitating and often fatal disease, in Swabia in the 1680s. This prompted me to make plans for a field trip to that region to look for evidence of outbreaks of the disease in the municipal archives of Ulm and other Swabian towns, and from my findings I learned what caused the *colica Pictonum* and how Eberhard Gockel discovered its cause.

As the city physician of Ulm, Gockel attended the monks in the town's two monasteries, most of whom had fallen victim to the disease. In a book he published later, Gockel noted that only those monks who drank wine had fallen ill, and at about the same time, while non-drinkers had been spared; he also noticed that his patients' symptoms were strikingly similar to those of the *Hüttenkatze*, the disease of lead workers which Samuel Stockhausen, the miners' physician in Goslar, had described in a recent book. Gockel was, moreover, offered a glass of wine each time he visited his monastic patients and he soon developed the same symptoms as they. He thereupon called on the vintner who supplied the wine to the monasteries and obtained from him his recipe for 'sweetening' and preserving wine. It bore striking resemblance to that for sapa, a syrup used for the same purpose in ancient Rome, which was prepared by boiling down must or wine in a leaden kettle. After returning to Bell Labs, I made sapa according to the detailed recipes in the Roman literature, and also, according to the vintner's recipe and was able to show that the lead content of these leaded wines explained the severity of symptoms they caused. These findings and an account of the history of lead disease over the centuries were published in *Medical History*, as well as in a number of popular science and history journals. (See http://www.ncbi.nlm.nih.gov/pmc/articles/PMC1139187/)

Following this very gratifying excursion into historical research, my interests returned to fluorescent molecules and their use for obtaining structural information. Cell membranes, though only two molecules in thickness, are remarkably complex structures that contain many different proteins that control the function of all cells. I collaborated with a Finnish biochemist who synthesized the specialized fluorescent molecules with which we investigated the fluid properties of model membranes, as well as biological cell membranes.

It was clear that more detailed information about dynamical properties of cells and membranes could be obtained by tracking the motion of individual molecules by means of a fluorescence microscope equipped with a sensitive imaging device. CCDs had just been invented at Bell Labs and had the requisite sensitivity but were not yet commercially available at that time. The few that were successfully manufactured were reserved for use in military satellites. My friend Tony Tyson, an astronomer, managed to scrounge a few CCDs from George E. Smith, the co-inventor of the CCD, whose lab was just down the hall. Tony used these early, crude CCDs (100 x 100 pixels in size) to construct a massive, liquid air-cooled CCD camera that he coupled to large telescopes in Chile and Hawaii and imaged the most distant galaxies of our universe with it. It was easy to convince Tony to let me borrow his camera and couple it to my fluorescence microscope. This allowed us to image fluorescent molecules inside biological cells, the first use of a CCD camera for investigating biological specimens labeled with fluorescent probes, which has since become a widely used experimental technique. It is also an example of the kind of collaborative research that was possible in the old Bell Labs. I took part in many collaborative studies with researchers at various universities and medical schools. At about that time, I also re-visited my physics roots by teaching a graduate course in atomic physics at New York University – conveniently located just a few blocks from our Houston Street home.

Until the 1980s Bell Labs had long been administered by scientists or engineers, but with AT&T facing growing competition, its policy was increasingly guided by the bottom line and the tradition of unfettered pure research eroded. The link between Bell Labs and its parent company AT&T weakened, and in time, it was severed. Many of the scientists in the basic research area drifted to universities, and when I was offered a professorship at Mount Sinai School of Medicine in 1986, I accepted and joined in the exodus.

At Mount Sinai I lectured on biophysics topics, mostly to MD/PhD students, who, I found were less well grounded in basic physics and mathematics than students of my era; on the other hand, they were adept at the use of computers, while we, as students, had made do with slide-rules and log tables. Occasionally, I also lectured to medical students on the history of medicine.

Together with my greatly-missed colleague and friend Massimo Sassaroli, whom I knew from our Bell Labs days, I founded, at Mount Sinai, the Cell Imaging Laboratory with its polyglot staff. With the aid of Heikki Väänänen, a brilliant, quirky Finn, we developed instrumentation for recording the movement of biological molecules labeled with fluorescent tracers – novel experiments at the time and routine today, with hundreds of fluorescent labels commercially available – and employed the technique in various collaborative research projects. In 1986, when my NIH application for renewed funding of the Cell Imaging Lab was unsuccessful, I had had my fill of writing research proposals and dealing with attendant politics, and withdrew into the enviable existence of a professor emeritus. Massimo took over the Cell Imaging Lab, but sadly, he died soon afterwards (2003).

* * *

At the beginning of my peripatetic career in science I paid little heed to the source of research funds and assumed, somewhat naively, that an enlightened society supported fundamental scientific research in the same way it supported other cultural activities. Unraveling the inner workings of nature was a role that suited my temperament and I deem myself fortunate for having had the opportunity to do so. My father could never understand why I was being paid handsomely for such work. In time, alas, the ivory tower that was Bell Labs crumbled, in part as a result of its own successes which led to its demise. The fruits of my research, published as 150 articles in professional journals and book chapters, added to the bulging edifice of our scientific knowledge: some of that research work formed the basis of subsequent research findings, some fell into oblivion, and some led to useful applications in medicine which – I like to think – enhanced human well-being.

The greatest satisfaction that I derived from my life in science is an awareness of the cosmic, physical, and biological evolutions, as well as an appreciation of the societal evolution that led to the chaotic world we now inhabit. These insights do not provide answers to the eternal existential questions, but they do offer intellectual gratification, even a certain solace, late in life.

I relish the sense of freedom that retirement brought, but the work habits of a lifetime are not easily discarded. Styra drew me into a number of historical research projects related to Johannes Brahms, the most important one being the transcription and translation of hundreds of Brahms's letters for Styra's *magnum opus: Johannes Brahms. Life and Letters* (Oxford University Press, 1997). My familiarity with the old German script (*Kurrent*) dating back my days at the Akademische Gymnasium seventy five years earlier, was finally put to good use. The best part of our collaboration were the European jaunts in which we followed the traces of Brahms from Hamburg to Vienna and many places in between. Her work has now been widely recognized and brought her many enjoyable perks, such as an invitation for both of us to spend two weeks in Brahms's summer residences in Lichtenthal near Baden-Baden (see my sketch).

For a while I was also re-connected to my work on lead disease of many years ago, when Styra persuaded me to investigate Beethoven's last illness and cause of death. I was able to refute the widely publicized, but ill-conceived and unsubstantiated theory that he had been lead-poisoned by his physician (Beethoven Journal, Vol. 23/1, 2008), but as is well known, even hard evidence rarely overcomes a lurid myth.

Some sixty years after I had been a member of the Mendel household in Toronto, I was interviewed by a researcher who was tracing the life history of the Mendel family. Our conversations brought back to mind those halcyon days of my youth in Canada and reminded me of the Mendels' friendship – particularly, Toni's friendship – with Albert Einstein. They also made me aware of Einstein's unpublished travel diaries housed in the Einstein archive at Princeton University, where I was soon reading his words in his own neat hand writing. The diaries record Einstein's experiences and his candid opinion on everything from physics, music, people, and politics and the idea of making them accessible to a wider public resulted in *Einstein on the Road* (Prometheus Books, 2011). The book is an account of Einstein's far-flung travels in the days of the Weimar Republic, and it was followed by another book, *Einstein at Home* (Prometheus Books, 2016) which is based on the reminiscences of the Einsteins' housekeeper in Berlin as recorded by a German historian of science. My work as an Einstein scholar led to many invitations for talks about different aspects of Einstein, and it rekindled my interest in physics and cosmology — where my commitment to science began so long ago.

New York, January 2014

NOTES

[1] The science behind the ZPP-hematofluorometer harks back to human evolution which took place when virtually all lead in the Earth's crust was strongly bound to sulfur, e.g. in galena (PbS). Since proteins evolved in the absence of free lead, their constituent amino acids included the sulfur containing cysteine. In a lead-free environment this presented no health problem, but when Neolithic humans learned to smelt lead some 10,000 years ago, man was exposed to free lead. When ingested or inhaled, Pb binds to the cysteine residues of many proteins, triggering the various deleterious symptoms of lead disease. See: *http://www.ncbi.nlm.nih.gov/pmc/articles/PMC1139187/*

[2] In 1985, the members of the cell imaging laboratory were born in Finland, Romania, Portugal, China, Israel, Austria, and Italy.

Our family, ca. 1981.